COMPASSION
FOR
HUMANITY
IN THE
JEWISH
TRADITION

COMPASSION FOR HUMANITY IN THE JEWISH TRADITION

DAVID SEARS

JASON ARONSON INC.
Northvale, New Jersey
Jerusalem

This book was set in 12 pt. Berkeley Oldstyle Book by Alabama Book Composition of Deatsville, Alabama.

10 9 8 7 6 5 4 3 2 1

Library of Congress Cataloging-in-Publication Data

Compassion for humanity in the Jewish tradition / [compiled and with introductions] by David Sears.
    p.   cm.
Includes bibliographical references and index.
ISBN 0–7657–9987–1 (alk. paper)
1. Respect for persons (Jewish law) 2. Caring—Religious aspects—Judaism. 3. Jews—Election, Doctrine of. 4. Interpersonal relations—Religious aspects—Judaism. 5. Noahide Laws. 6. Ethics, Jewish. I. Sears, David.
BJ1286.R47S43 1998
296.3'117—dc21
                                                              97–33196
                                                                  CIP
                                                                  r97

Manufactured in the United States of America. Jason Aronson Inc. offers books and cassettes. For information and catalog write to Jason Aronson Inc., 230 Livingston Street, Northvale, New Jersey 07647.

Rafi Estrin

(Raphael Yitzhak Ephraim ben Aryeh Leib Shlom

6 Menachem Av 5735/1975 - 8 Elul 5757/1997)

In his brief twenty-two years,

Rafi brought light into the lives of all who knew him,

and brought the whole world a little closer to the Light.

For the sake of my brothers and friends
I shall speak of peace among you.

Psalms 122:8

Contents

Preface   xiii
Acknowledgments   xvii

1   **JUDAISM AND NON-JEWS**   1
     Sources   1
     Respect for All   1
     Love Thy Neighbor   6
     Reverence for Life   10
     The Family of Man   11
     Blessings of Non-Jews   13
     A Lesson from an Idol-Worshiper   15
     Fellow Travelers   16
     A Real Rabbi   17
     Racial Equality   19
     Moses as Social Activist   20
     Freedom for All   22
     Divine Compassion   23
     Sustainer of All   26
     Paths of Peace   27
     The Patriarchs and Humanity   35
     Good Citizenship   37
     Honesty in Business   41

Elijah's Rebuke   47
Measure for Measure   48
Fairness Toward One's Employees   49
A Master of Accounts   50
One Standard   52
Comic Justice   54
Righteous Non-Jews   55
The Crown of Torah   59
The Righteous Proselyte   63
The Sages and the High Priest   70
Maimonides' Letter to Obadiah
   the Righteous Convert   71
Seeking Proselytes   74
King Solomon's Prayer   77
The Holy Temple   78
Jerusalem   79
Enlightenment   83
Abraham's Other Son   86
Non-Jews in the Holy Land   88
Other Religions   90
Tikkun Olam: Perfecting the World   93
Exile and Redemption   98
Return to God   100
Divine Service   102
Disseminating the Seven Laws of
   Noah   103
Chasidic Teachings for Non-Jews   105
A Universal Message   106
Post-Holocaust Universalism   107
A Common Accord   109

2   **THE CHOSEN PEOPLE**   **111**
Introduction   **111**
Sources   **117**
Not Because You Were Greater   117
The Divine Witness   118

Universal Benefit   119
The Heart of the World   120
Dedication to God   121
Suffering for Humanity   122
All Nations Are Beloved   124
Between Heaven and Earth   126
Jethro's Wisdom   129
In Their Merit   130
Why Israel Is Called "Adam"   131
Dedication to God   137
Higher than Mind   138
Brotherhood of Mankind   139
Unity in Diversity   141
Dedication to Mankind   142

3   THE MESSIANIC VISION   145
    Introduction   145
    Sources   152
    A Light unto the Nations   159

ESSAYS   163

4   THE SEVEN UNIVERSAL LAWS OF NOAH   165

5   THE MERCIFUL ONE DESIRES THE HEART   175

6   TEFILLIN: PARADIGM OF UNITY   183

7   PRAYERS   189
    Introduction   189
    Sources   191
    Rabbi Nosson's Prayers   193

Afterword   197
Biographies   199
Related Reading   219
Index   221

Preface

Early in life, almost everyone who went to public school in America learned that "all men are created equal," and that when people think otherwise, the results are usually tragic. For most of us, universalism is the cornerstone of our morality. Therefore, the biblical designation of the Jews as God's "treasured nation" or "chosen people" is disturbing. How could a benevolent Creator who formed all of humanity from a common ancestor elevate one nation seemingly to the exclusion of the rest? How could the Giver of the Torah which rebukes the Patriarch Jacob for favoring one son above the others (*Shabbos* 10b) behave the same way toward His own children?

For those who did not go to public schools but *yeshivos*— Jewish religious schools—these questions might not be so pressing. Instead, universalism itself is suspect. The Torah describes the Jews as "a people who shall dwell alone and shall not be reckoned among the nations" (Numbers 23:9). Much of Jewish law is devoted to the specific spiritual practices and obligations that preserve the Jewish community as a survival unit in a sea of shifting historical circumstances. Moreover, the ancient rabbis compare Israel to "a sheep surrounded by seventy wolves,"[1] and

---

1. *Tanchuma, Toldos* 5; *Pesikta Rabbasi* 9:3.

two thousand years of exile have generally vindicated their way of sizing things up. Who considers the virtues of universalism when the Cossacks are kicking down the door? In any case, isn't the main point of Judaism its particularism? Thus, the average Torah-observant Jew feels that it is sufficient to go his own way, the way of Torah, until the Messiah comes and brings the long night of exile to an end.

Although most of the texts cited here are not obscure, this anthology may contain some news for many readers, secularists and Torah-observant Jews alike. It demonstrates that the Jewish people were indeed chosen, but not merely to sustain themselves as fugitives of history. Instead, the Torah instructs the Israelites to be a "light unto the nations," a model of spirituality and moral refinement that will inspire the rest of the world to turn to God of its own accord. This is one of the main forms of *kiddush Hashem*—sanctification of God's name.

In order for the Jews to maintain the purity of their ideal, it is necessary for them to resist assimilation, socially and intellectually. Many of the Torah's precepts underscore the uniqueness of the Jewish people and the role they play in fulfilling the Divine plan. As a living testimony to the existence of God, the Jews are commanded to maintain their uniqueness without compromise. Additionally, during the Syrian–Greek and Roman occupations of Israel, the rabbis enacted many decrees precisely to impede the easy mingling of Jews and non-Jews. Their formula for the survival of the Jewish people as a conquered nation and, later, as a minority group struggling to maintain its identity demonstrates great wisdom and foresight. The resultant insularity of Torah-observant communities has, at times, led to misunderstanding and animosity. However, the ultimate goal of this particularism is to benefit all of humanity and all of creation. This has been the great spiritual task of the Jews, both in their own land and in the many lands of their diaspora.

To be sure, Israel has not always succeeded in fulfilling this Divinely appointed mission. For this reason the Jewish people are compared to the moon, which wanes almost to the point of

extinction and then waxes large again.[2] When we succumb to
material pursuits, our light is diminished. When we maintain our
ideal, we remain strong, and our light shines to all. When the
Holy Temple in Jerusalem was destroyed by Rome and the last
and longest exile of the Jewish people began, the nation almost
despaired of its future. However, some two thousand years later,
we find that the Torah's teachings have influenced societies all
over the world. And, despite a long succession of dire predictions, the Jewish people have outlived all those who sought their
extinction.[3]

The intent of this work is not to convince the reader of any
point of Jewish dogma. Rather, we wish to delineate certain
universalist and humanist components of Judaism. The material
we have chosen is firmly rooted in the rabbinic tradition, without
recourse to more contemporary apologetics. The source-texts are
classics of traditional Jewish thought, from Scripture through
the Talmud and up to contemporary rabbinic leaders. Almost
the entire spectrum of world Jewry is represented: Sephardim
(Middle Eastern Jews) and Ashkenazim (European Jews), Chasidim and non-Chasidim. (It should also be understood that these
selections reflect a limited range of opinions within the tradition.
Therefore, this work should be considered a starting point, not
the final word, on any subject it mentions.) For all those who
identify with Judaism or who wish to better understand the
"People of the Book," this anthology may answer some basic
questions. These answers may not be congenial to everyone, but
it is hoped that they will promote a spirit of tolerance between
those of differing world views. At the very least they should
dispel some of the suspicion and even hatred that have too often
insinuated themselves into religion, the main purpose of which is
to bring peace to the world.

---

2. *Likkutei Halachos, Hilchos Tefillin* 5:19; ibid., *Rosh Chodesh* 4; ibid., *Eidus*
5:13–14; ibid., *Nefilas Apayim* 4:20.

3. See Rabbi Mannaseh Ben Israel, "The Conciliator," on Isaiah 52:8.

Acknowledgments

Many people shared in bringing this work to completion. I am grateful to my revered teacher, Rabbi Elazar Mordechai Kenig, *shlita*, of Kiryat Breslev, Tzefat, Israel, for his continual encouragement, guidance, and blessings. I must also thank an old friend, Fishel Bresler, for first inspiring this project. He also proved to be an excellent editor—as did Arthur Kurzweil, vice president of Jason Aronson Inc. It was a pleasure to work with production editor Dana Salzman, designer Judith Tulli and the rest of the Jason Aronson staff. Rabbi Shmuel Teich, the Pshemishler Rebbe, *shlita*, Rabbi Shlomo Aharon Gottleib of Jerusalem's Breslov Kollel, Rabbi Myer Fund of the Flatbush Minyan, and Rabbi Yaacov Haber of the Pardes Project were kind enough to review this manuscript in its various stages of development. My long-time *chavrusos*, Rabbi Symcha Bergman and David Zeitlin, read sections of the manuscript and made a number of useful suggestions, as did Rabbi Eliezer Shore, Nachman Futterman, Leibel Estrin, and Andy Statman. The essays were edited by Rabbi Zvi Davis, head of Ateres Moshe Aharon, and my son, Yonah Eliyahu Sears. Rabbi Aharon Yonah Hayum of the Bostoner Kollel Haichal HaFla'ah looked over most of the translations and source references (although responsibility for any mistakes rests with me), and Yaakov David Shulman co-translated one of the selections from Rav Kook. I am especially grateful to my parents,

Dr. and Mrs. Lewis Sears, for imparting through their word and example the values espoused by this book, and my wife, Shira Sara, for her encouragement and patience. Most of all, I would like to thank God for enabling me to complete this work.

The following authors and publishers kindly permitted us to reprint excerpts from their works: Rabbi Samson Raphael Hirsch, *Judaism Eternal* (Soncino), *Commentary on the Pentateuch* (Judaica), *The Hirsch Psalms* (Feldheim), and *The Nineteen Letters* (Feldheim); Rabbi Shimon Finkelman, *Reb Moshe: The Life and Ideals of HaGaon Rabbi Moshe Feinstein* (Artscroll/Mesorah); Rabbi Elie Munk, *Ascent to Harmony* (Feldheim); Bezalel Naor, *Of Societies Perfect and Imperfect: Selected Readings from Eyn Ayah, Rav Kook's Commentary to Eyn Yaakov* (Sepher-Hermon); Rabbi Chaim Efraim Zaitchik, *Sparks of Mussar* (Feldheim); Rabbi Jonathan Sacks, *Tradition in an Untraditional Age* (Vallentine, Mitchell); Rabbi Ahron Soloveitchik, *The Warmth and the Light* (Genesis/ Jerusalem), *Logic of the Heart, Logic of the Mind* (Genesis/ Jerusalem). Additionally, we are grateful to the Heichal Menachem Library of Borough Park, the Kehot Publishing Society, and Sichos In English, whose publications we consulted in preparing our own translations from the works of the late Lubavitcher Rebbe. Similarly, we consulted Rabbi Mendel Hirsch's *The Haftoroth* (Judaica) in the course of preparing our own versions of his commentary. Two important sources of biographical information were Rabbi Hirsh Goldwurm's *The Rishonim* and *The Early Acharonim* (Artscroll/Mesorah). These works are based upon the research of Rabbi Shmuel Teich, the Pshemishler Rebbe, *shlita*, who also provided additional information for the present volume. *Acharon acharon chaviv*, we thank Rabbi Levi Yitzchak Horowitz, the Bostoner Rebbe, *shlita*, who kindly allowed us to reprint an excerpt from his essay, "And You Shall Tell Your Son."

1

Judaism and Non-Jews

SOURCES

Respect for All

Ben Zoma used to say: Who is wise? One who learns from all people (*Mishna: Avos* 4:1).

༄

[Ben Azzai] used to say: Do not regard anyone with contempt, and do not reject anything, for there is no man who does not have his hour and nothing that does not have its place (*Mishna: Avos* 4:3).

༄

[Rabbi Chaninah Ben Dosa] used to say: Whoever is pleasing to his fellow creatures is pleasing to God; but whoever is not pleasing to his fellow creatures, God is not pleased with him (*Mishna: Avos* 3:10).

Commentary: The Mishna uses the term "fellow creatures," not the members of one's own nation, in order to include all mankind and all creatures, whether of one's own nation or another, whether an individual or a group. Our rabbis have clearly stated that there is no difference in this regard between Jews and non-Jews (Rabbi Pinchas Eliyahu of Vilna, *Sefer HaBris* II, 13:6).

Rabbi Yochanan said: Whoever speaks wisdom, although he is a non-Jew, is a Sage (*Talmud: Megilla* 16a).

Commentary: It is proper for a person to speak words of honor and respect concerning any Sage, even if he belongs to another nation (Rabbi Menachem Meiri, ad loc.).

If someone tells you that other nations possess wisdom, believe him. However, if someone tells you that other nations possess Torah, do not believe him (*Midrash: Eichah Rabba* 2:13).

One verse states, "You have not acted according to the ordinances of the nations surrounding you" (Ezekiel 5:7), whereas another verse states, "And you have acted according to the ordinances of the nations surrounding you" (Ezekiel 11:12). How is this possible? Their good practices you have not followed, but their evil practices you have followed (*Talmud: Sanhedrin* 39b).

A person should always be pleasant to all human beings, hastening to offer them greetings, and seeking their honor and benefit to the best of one's ability. This will cause one to be beloved by others, and inspire them to honor the Torah and its precepts (Rabbi Menachem Meiri on *Berachos* 6b).

[One should] respect all creatures, recognizing in them the greatness of the Creator who formed man with wisdom, and whose wisdom is contained in all creatures. He should realize that they greatly deserve to be honored, since the Former of All Things, the Wise One who is exalted above all, cared to create them. If one despises them, God forbid, it reflects upon the honor of their Creator.

This may be likened to an expert goldsmith who fashions a vessel with great skill, but when he displays his work, one of the people begins to mock and scorn it. How angry that goldsmith will be; for by disparaging his handiwork, one disparages his wisdom. Similarly, it is evil in the sight of the Holy One, blessed be He, if any of His creatures is despised.

This is [the meaning of] the verse, "How many are your works, O Lord" (Psalms 104:24). [The Psalmist] did not say "how vast" but "how many." [The Hebrew word *rav*—"many"—also denotes importance,] as in the phrase, "*rav beiso*," (*Megillas Esther* 1:8), meaning "of high status." Since You imbued them all with Your wisdom, Your works are important and great, and it befits one to contemplate the wisdom in them and not disparage them (Rabbi Moshe Cordovero, *Tomer Devorah*, chap. 2).

It is written, "You shall rise up before the hoary head and honor the face of the elder" (Leviticus 19:32). The expression "elder" refers to one versed in the Torah, as it is written, "Gather unto Me seventy of the elders of Israel" (Numbers 11:16). And there the choice was surely made on the basis of wisdom, not age, as it is written, "Whom you know to be the elders of the people and its officers" (Numbers 11:16). Therefore, it is mandatory to revere and honor one who is learned in Torah, even if he is not advanced in years, and even if he is not one's own teacher. [However,] it is also mandatory to respect and honor a person seventy years or older, even if he is unlearned, provided that he is not an evildoer. An elderly non-Jew should likewise be shown respect by kind words and by being given a helping hand (Rabbi Shlomo Ganzfried, *Kitzur Shulchan Aruch* 144:2).

It is forbidden to show ingratitude, whether to a Jew or a non-Jew (Rabbi Nachman of Breslov, *Sefer HaMidos, Tefilah* 62).

All human beings are precious, be they Jews or non-Jews, for they were created in the image of God. Rabbi Nosson Zvi [Finkel, also known as the Alter of Slobodka,] showed honor and *chesed* (kindness) to them all. On a walk through Slobodka with his son-in-law, Rabbi Isaac, Rabbi Nosson Zvi was delighted to notice that a coffeehouse for non-Jews had opened near the highway. "Until now," he said, "I used to worry that travelers had no place near the road to eat and rest. Now they will be able to eat and rest as soon as they arrive in the city" (Rabbi Chaim Ephraim Zaitchik, *Sparks of Mussar*).

Whenever a guest left his house, Rabbi Nosson Zvi escorted him outside. When he was in a German spa, he used to accompany the trains leaving the place in order to fulfill the *mitzvah* (Divine commandment) of escort. Once a caravan of Gypsies passed by, and he accompanied them, too (ibid.).

The root of the obligation to be considerate is our obligation to a person because he is a person (Rabbi Eliyahu Dessler, *Michtav M'Eliyahu* IV, p. 246).

Love Thy Neighbor

Love of one's neighbor means that we should love all people, no matter to which nation they belong or what language they speak. For all men are created in the Divine image, and all engage in improving civilization, whether by building, ploughing, planting, or business, by physical labor or by advancing human wisdom to benefit the world, so that no one should remain disadvantaged. Man makes the world habitable with his wisdom. He studies, searches, and develops tools and wondrous inventions through his intellectual exertion. By such things the world stands and is perfected. Thus, "everything which the Lord created [for man] to do" (Genesis 2:3) and "which He accomplished, and, behold, it was very good" (Genesis 1:31) may be available to all humanity.

Our love of humanity should take no exception to any nation or individual. For man was not created for his own sake exclusively; rather, all men exist for the sake of one another. As a sage once said, "The world and all it contains was created for mankind, and within mankind itself, one person was created for the sake of the next, each one to benefit the other." Therefore, not only does [love of one's fellow] apply to the Jewish people but to all mankind. We should love all nations and include all peoples in this universal principle, "the stranger and the native son" alike, all who inhabit the earth.

Let every man strive for the benefit of his fellow, in a spirit of mutuality, whether in physical concerns or in financial matters, for the collective good and for the improvement of society. Loving one's neighbor means that we should befriend all human beings (Rabbi Pinchas Eliyahu of Vilna, *Sefer HaBris*, sect. II, discourse 13).

It can be demonstrated by scriptural proof [that the Divine commandment of loving one's neighbor extends to both Jews and non-Jews]. God clearly imposed it upon His people, and the Torah clearly obligates us in this matter: "And you shall love your neighbor as yourself" (Leviticus 19:18). The intent of this verse is not to limit [the performance of the precept] to Israel exclusively. If this were the case, it would have said, "You shall love your brother as yourself," as it states concerning usury, "You shall not pay interest to your brother" (Deuteronomy 23:20). Or it would have said, "You shall love the members of your people as yourself," as it states, "You shall not take vengeance against those of your people" (Leviticus 19:18).

The intent of the term "your neighbor" is to indicate a person like yourself, who participates in civilization like yourself, and this denotes members of all nations. Our Sages did not understand the term "your neighbor" in this verse to delimit our neighborly love from the nations of the world. For it is axiomatic that our Sages never interpreted anything, whether to limit or increase, according to their own whim. Only if they possessed a tradition that this was the specific intent of a scriptural verse did they so interpret it, whether to limit or increase, and in no other context, even if the same word or expression occurs frequently throughout the Torah.

Moreover, there is a scriptural verse where a non-Jew is also called "neighbor," as it states, "Chushai the Arkite, David's friend" (II Samuel 16:16). [The Hebrew word for "friend" can also mean "neighbor."] And our Sages state that "Chushai was a non-Jew like Ittai the Gitite, who accompanied David when he fled from Absalam, his son" (II Samuel 15:19). (ibid., 13:5).

All the commandments between man and man are included in the precept of loving one's neighbor. As we have said, that is the true path by which to attain Divine Inspiration. It is written of Rabbi Yosef [Saragossi], teacher of Rabbi David Ben Zimra, that by virtue of his love of all humanity, he received a spiritual visitation of the Prophet Elijah—and to behold Elijah's pure countenance is like gazing upon the face of God and His angels. Thus, we have also discussed this precept in the discourse, "On the Mystery of Divine Inspiration," where it mentions the commandments between man and God which enable a person to attain Divine Inspiration (ibid., 13:31).

Once someone mentioned a certain holy book to the Chassidic master Rabbi Pinchas of Koretz, which states that one must also love non-Jews because they are God's creatures. It seems to me that this was the *Sefer HaBris* (cited above). Rabbi Pinchas was extremely pleased with this teaching (*Imrei Pinchas, Inyanim Shonim* 79).

[The character traits necessary for a person to experience attachment to God are] self-effacement to the utmost degree; not to succumb to anger, even with the members of one's household; not to be the least bit resentful [of any insult or slight]; to be among those who are disparaged and do not respond in like manner; and to love all creatures, including non-Jews (Rabbi Chaim Vital, *Sha'arei Kedushah* I:5).

Love of all creatures is also love of God, for whoever loves the One loves all the works that He has made. When one loves God, it is impossible not to love His creatures. [Also, the converse is true.] If one hates the creatures, it is impossible to love God Who created them (Maharal of Prague, *Nasivos Olam*, Ahavas HaRe'i, 1).

Love of all creatures requires great effort, that it may be broadened to the fullest extent. Due to our lack of experience, this love may appear to be a matter of little importance, even contrary to the Torah and common ethics. However, [in truth,] it must constantly fill all the chambers of the soul.

The highest level of our love for all creatures must be the love of humanity, which should extend to all its members. Despite the differences of religion and ideology, despite the differences of race and environment, one should try to understand the mentality of the various nations and factions as much as possible, in order to appreciate their character and nature. Then one can know how to base the love of humanity on foundations that lead to actual deed.

Only when the soul is enriched by the love of all creatures and all humanity can the love of [Israel] be elevated to its lofty station and attain greatness, both in spirit and in practice. It is a mean eye that causes one to see only ugliness and impurity in everything beyond the bounds of Israel, the unique nation. This is one of the most awful, debased forms of darkness. It damages the entire edifice of spiritual virtue, the light of which every sensitive soul seeks (Rabbi Avraham Yitzchak Kook, manuscript cited in *Mishnato Shel HaRav Kook*, pp. 306–307).

Reverence for Life

Divine Wisdom gives life to all things, as it is written, "Wisdom gives life to all who possess it" (Ecclesiastes 7:12). Thus, one should instruct the entire world in the ways of life, helping others to attain life in this world and in the World to Come and providing them with the means to life. As a matter of principle, one should give life to all beings.

Moreover, Divine Wisdom is the "father" of all that exists.[1] As the verse states, "How many are Your works, O Lord; You have made them all with wisdom" (Psalms 104:24). Thus, everything that lives and exists comes from this source. Similarly, a person should act as a father to all of God's creatures, particularly Israel, whose holy souls emanate from [the Divine thought]. At all times, one should beseech God's mercy and blessing for the world, emulating our Father above, who has compassion for His creatures (Rabbi Moshe Cordovero, *Tomer Devorah*, chap. 3).

---

1. In Kabbalistic literature, the Divine attribute of Wisdom (*chochmah*) is personified as a father (*abba*), whereas the Divine attribute of understanding (*binah*) is personified as a mother (*imah*).

The Family of Man

Adam was created alone in order that peace should prevail among all creatures; for no one can say, "My father is greater than your father" (*Talmud: Sanhedrin* 37a).

[Rabbi Akiva] used to say: Beloved is Man, for he was created in the Divine image. It is an even greater [act of] love that it was made known to him that he was created in the Divine image, as it states, "In the image of God was man created" (Genesis 1:27) (*Mishna: Avos* 3:14).

Commentary 1: Rabbi Akiva spoke of all mankind, citing the scriptural verse that refers to the descendants of Noah, and not the Israelites alone. Rabbi Akiva wished to confer merit upon all people, including the descendants of Noah [who uphold the Seven Universal Laws] (*Tosefos Yom Tom*, ad loc.).

Commentary 2: It seems to me that the text of the Mishna should be emended to state *ha-adam*—"man" with the definite article—to include non-Jews. This distinction is discussed in the Talmudic glosses of Tosefos on tractate *Yevamos* 61a. Also, since the Mishna concludes, "Beloved is Israel . . ." it may be inferred that the first section, by contrast, refers to all mankind. Likewise, the scriptural proof cited above [by Rabbi Akiva], "God created man in the Divine image," refers to the descendants of Noah. This includes non-Jews, as Tosefos Yom Tov states in his commentary (ad loc.). Another proof is that when Joshua killed Ai and the other five kings [during the conquest of Canaan], he did not allow their bodies to remain hanging after nightfall (*Joshua* 8:29, 10:27). [The Torah forbids treating the human body disrespectfully because it was created in the Divine image.] Thus, it may be deduced that non-Jews also possess it (Rabbi Yisrael Lifshutz, *Tiferes Yisrael* (*Yachin*) on *Avos* 3:14).

Blessings of Non-Jews

Rabbi Tanchuma taught: If an idol-worshiper blesses you, say "amen" afterwards. Thus it is written, "You shall be blessed above (*mikol*) all the nations" (Deuteronomy 7:14). [Rabbi Tanchuma renders the verse homiletically to mean, "You shall be blessed by (*mikol*) all the nations." However, this does not refer to blessings in the name of other deities] (*Midrash: Bereishis Rabba, Toldos* 66:6).

Do not think that the blessing of a non-Jew is of little worth (Rabbi Nachman of Breslov, *Sefer HaMidos, Beracha* 2).

"Rabbi [Yehudah HaNasi] used to say: Which is the right path that a person should choose for himself? That which is honorable to himself and which brings him honor from mankind" (*Mishna: Avos* 2:1).

Commentary: "That which is honorable to himself" points to the potential of human beings to unite with God without intermediaries. After a person has thoroughly developed his required connection to God through the Torah, he should also seek to develop an intimate, private relationship with God. Nevertheless, the connection with God a person establishes must also bring him "honor from mankind." Coming close to God

13

must not take one away from the world. [As the Talmud states in *Kiddushin* 40a,] a person's conduct should be "good to the heavens and good to the creations"; that is, the good one does should be felt by others. While striving for the spiritual heights, a person must find favor in the eyes of his fellow men, Jews and non-Jews alike (Rabbi Menachem M. Schneerson of Lubavitch, *Sefer HaSichos* 5750, vol. II, p. 420ff.; ibid., 5751, vol. II, p. 497ff.).

A Lesson from an Idol-Worshiper

Rabbi Yehudah said in the name of Rabbi Shmuel: Rabbi Eliezer was asked to what lengths a person must go to fulfill the commandment of honoring one's father and mother. He answered: "A worshiper of the stars in Ashkelon—Dama Ben Nesina by name—was once approached by the Sages of Israel, who wished to buy a certain jewel from him for the breastplate of the Kohen Gadol (High Priest). They offered him 600,000 gold coins—Rav Kahana said they offered 800,000—but the key [to the safe in which the jewel was kept] was under his [sleeping] father's head, and [Dama Ben Nesina] would not disturb him."

Another version [of this tradition] states that the Holy One, blessed be He, rewarded him by causing a red heifer to be born to his herd. [Desiring this animal for the service of the Holy Temple,] the Sages came before him. "I know you," he said. "If I asked you for all the wealth in the world, you would give it to me. However, I asked you only for the money I lost for the sake of my father's honor." When the Sages heard about this, they said: "If this was the reward of one who fulfilled a precept concerning which he was not commanded, how much greater is the reward of one who is commanded and obeys" (*Talmud: Kiddushin* 31a).

Fellow Travelers

Once the Talmudic Sage Rabbi Pinchas Ben Ya'ir was on his way to ransom several Jews from captivity. He came to the river Ginnai and could not procede. "O Ginnai," he cried, "divide your waters for me, that I may cross over!" The river replied, "You are about to perform the will of your Maker, and so am I. You may or may not accomplish your purpose. However, I will surely accomplish mine." [Rabbi Pinchas] replied, "If you will not divide yourself, I shall decree that your waters cease to flow forever." It thereupon divided itself for him.

There was another man with him who was transporting wheat for the festival of Passover. Once again, Rabbi Pinchas addressed the river, "Divide yourself for this man, too, since he is engaged in a religious duty." It divided itself for him as well.

Also, an Arab had come along with them for the journey. Rabbi Pinchas addressed the river, "Divide your waters for him, too. Shall he rebuke us by saying, 'Is this how you treat a fellow traveler?'" The river divided itself again (*Talmud: Chullin* 7a).

A Real Rabbi

[The Jewish] chaplain at Maimonides Medical Center in New York once addressed a group of nurses and, in the course of his remarks, mentioned Reb Moshe [Feinstein]'s name. "Oh!" exclaimed a black nurse named Shirley, "I know Rabbi Feinstein. He's a real rabbi!"

[The chaplain] could not imagine how the woman could know Reb Moshe and told her that she must be confusing him with someone else. No, Shirley insisted, there was no mistake. She was speaking of the famous Rabbi Feinstein. She had been the house-nurse for one of Reb Moshe's newborn great-grandsons, at whose *bris* (circumcision) Reb Moshe had served as *sandek*.[2] As he was wheeled out following the *bris*, Rabbi Moshe made a point of turning around in his wheelchair to say good-bye to the nurse. This show of respect had made an indelible impression on her.

This same nurse called on Reb Moshe's family after his passing to express her condolences. "I remember how the Rabbi smiled and wished me a good day," she recalled. "I could see that in his eyes I was important" (Rabbi Shimon Finkleman, *Reb Moshe*, chap. 7, pp. 155–156).

The dignity of all creatures formed in the Divine image is not limited to the Jewish people alone. There was an old Russian

---

2. The *sandek* is the person on whose lap the infant rests during the ritual of circumcision.

caretaker in Tiferes Jerusalem [Rabbi Moshe Feinstein's rabbinical academy on New York's Lower East Side]. His English was poor, so no one paid much attention to him. One day he developed a painful toothache and appeared with a handkerchief wrapped around his chin. When Rabbi Moshe came upon him in the anteroom, he stopped in order to speak with him [in Russian] for several minutes. When the conversation came to an end, the caretaker turned to leave. On his face was a wide smile of contentment (ibid., Hebrew ed. p. 123).

Racial Equality

From the standpoint of the Torah there can be no distinction between one human being and another on the basis of race or color. Any discrimination shown to another human being on account of the color of his or her skin constitutes loathsome barbarity. It must be conceded that the Torah recognizes a distinction between a Jew and a non-Jew. This distinction, however, is not based upon race, origin, or color, but rather upon *k'dushah*, the holiness endowed by having been given and having accepted the Torah. Furthermore, the distinction between Jew and non-Jew does not involve any concept of inferiority but is based primarily upon the unique and special burdens that are incumbent upon the Jews (Rabbi Ahron Soloveitchik, *Logic of the Heart, Logic of the Mind*, chap. 5, Civil Rights and the Dignity of Man).

Moses as Social Activist

At the beginning of Exodus, the Torah relates three episodes in Moses's life before God designated him the deliverer of the Jews from Egypt. On the first day that Moses went out to his people from the house of Pharaoh, where he was raised, he saw an Egyptian striking a Hebrew. Here the outstanding quality of Moses first reveals itself. With an overwhelming passion for justice and righteousness, the inability to tolerate a crime, Moses hastily looked around and rushed forward to defend the Hebrew against the Egyptian aggressor. This, the first act in Moses's life as a grown-up, represents part of the *tzedek* (justice and righteousness) that is to be realized in the realm of Gentile-versus-Jew relationships. But then the Torah tells us that Moses went out again and this time saw one Jew smiting another. Moses rushed to the aid of the victim, defending him against the aggressor. This second act of Moses represents his dedication to the cause of justice and righteousness in the realm of Jew-versus-Jew relationships. As a result of this second act, however, Moses was forced to flee Egypt. The once-pampered Egyptian prince of the royal household became a homeless, hunted refugee.

Moses comes to a well where he witnesses another act of injustice. The local shepherds drive away the shepherd daughters of Jethro, so that the shepherds can water their flocks first. Here Moses enters a dispute between non-Jews, a matter seemingly so unimportant to him that we might have understood had he stood idly by. Hadn't he learned his bitter lesson already? Did not discretion urge him to "mind his own business"?

Our Sages say, "Moses represents *tzedek*" (*Midrash Rabbah, Shemos*). The concept of *tzedek*, as we have begun to develop, is to be pursued in three different realms. First, as Moses taught us, a Jew must be on guard not to allow injustice in the relationship of a non-Jew with a Jew. Second, a Jew must be careful that justice be shown in relationships between Jews. Third, the incident by the well in Midian teaches us that Moses was bent upon emulating the ways of God, one of which is to defend a victim from an attacker, as the verse says, "God takes the side of the aggrieved and the victim" (Ecclesiastes 3:15). In Moses's mind, the pursuit of righteousness and justice was paramount; no consideration could stand in its way—"And Moses stood up and helped them and watered their flocks" (Exodus 2:17). A Jew should always identify with the cause of defending the aggrieved, whosoever the aggrieved may be, just as the concept of *tzedek* is to be applied uniformly to all humans, regardless of race or creed (Rabbi Ahron Soloveitchik, *Logic of the Heart, Logic of the Mind*, chap. 5, Civil Rights and the Dignity of Man).

Freedom for All

The fact that the Jewish people had to experience "four hundred years of Egyptian exile, including 210 years of actual slavery" (Rashi on Genesis 15:13) was critical in molding our national personality into one of compassion and concern for our fellow man, informed by the realization that we have a vital role to play in this world. For this reason, God begins the Ten Commandments with a reminder that "I am the Lord, your God, who took you out of Egypt" (Exodus 20:2). We must constantly remember that we ourselves were slaves in order to always appreciate the ideal of freedom, not only for ourselves but also for others. We must do what we can to help others to live free of the bondage of the evil spirit, free of the bondage of cruelty, of abuse, and of a lack of caring (Rabbi Levi Yitzchak Horowitz, Bostoner Rebbe, And You Shall Tell Your Son. *Young Israel Viewpoint*, Spring 1997).

Divine Compassion

God is good to all, and His mercy extends to all of His creatures (*Psalms* 145:9).

Commentary: Every king shows kindness to a few select individuals; God alone is good to all. Also, a mortal king shows mercy only to his beloved servants; God alone has mercy upon all His creatures (Rabbi Abraham ibn Ezra, ad loc.).

All the prophets of Israel had mercy on both the Israelites and the gentile nations. Thus, Jeremiah bewailed the calamity of Moab (Jeremiah 48:31–47). Similarly, Ezekiel lamented the sufferings of Tyre (Ezekiel 27). [Isaiah, too, grieved over the misfortune of other nations] (*Midrash: Bamidbar Rabba* 20:1).

"And shall I not have pity upon Nineveh, that great city which has more than 120,000 people who do not know their right hand from their left, and also many animals?" (Jonah 4:11).

Commentary: "And shall I not have pity upon Nineveh," whose inhabitants are the work of My hand? "That great city" is an expression of endearment. Despite the fact that idolatry is prevalent there, [Nineveh] contains "more than 120,000 people who do not know their right hand from their left." That is, they lack the knowledge to distinguish between the service of the One

God, which is figuratively associated with the right side, and the service associated with the left side, the deification of nature or astrological forces. [God does] not punish them for their lack of knowledge. "And also many animals." If a person sins, in what does an animal sin? This also explains why Israel is punished. The Jewish people already learned to distinguish between right and left, for they received the Divine law and the true faith. Israel deserves to be punished for idolatry, even though Nineveh was not punished for this (Rabbi Meir Leib Malbim, ad loc.).

God transcends and encompasses the universe; at the same time, God imbues the universe with life. In truth, everything that exists possesses the ability to recognize the Creator according to its nature and spiritual level: living beings (whether or not they possess the faculty of speech), vegetation—even inanimate objects. Every creature longs for God, and God cares for every creature. Therefore, God made the earth a sphere, to teach us that all the earth's inhabitants should feel equally close to Him (Rabbi Chaim ibn Attar, *Ohr HaChaim*, Genesis 2:1).

The Torah relates that the Patriarch Isaac dug three wells: Eisek, Sitna, and Rechovos (Genesis 26:20–22). It could be said that these wells correspond to the three festivals of Passover, Shavuos, and Succos. Passover commemorates the exodus from Egypt, when the Jewish people struggled (*eisek*) to be saved from their evil oppressors. [This corresponds to Eisek, the first well.] Shavuos commemorates the Giving of the Torah at Mount Sinai. Our Sages comment that the name Sinai alludes to the hatred (*sinah*) that the Jewish people have endured ever since (*Shabbos* 89b). [This corresponds to Sitna, the second well.] However, on Succos seventy sacrifices were offered on behalf of the nations of the world in order to promote peace. This corresponds to

Rechovos, the third well [whose name means "expansiveness" or "relief"].

Also, during this festival Heaven apportions the livelihood and sustenance of the entire world. The verse states, "Behold, I have given you every herb yielding seed which is upon the face of the earth, and every tree whose fruit yields seed; to you shall it be for food" (Genesis 1:29). For all creation was brought into being only so that the Holy One, blessed be He, may benefit His creatures, "for He desires kindness" (Micah 7:18). God's deepest desire is to have a fit receiver for His blessings. Therefore, "Behold, I have given . . ." is the last of the Ten Divine Sayings in the biblical account of creation and is followed by the declaration, "And God saw all that He had made, and, behold, it was very good" (Genesis 1:31). This act of giving is God's deepest desire. Therefore, [the festival of Succos, when sustenance is apportioned to the entire world,] is a time of great rejoicing above (Rabbi Yehudah Aryeh Leib Alter of Ger, *S'fas Emes, Inyan Succos*, p. 101a).

Sustainer of All

According to the Talmud (*Berachos* 48b), Moses composed the following blessing in gratitude for the manna with which God sustained the Israelites throughout their wanderings in the desert. It comprises the first section of the Grace After Meals, which the Jew must recite after eating bread. Although only Jews are obligated in its recitation, this blessing clearly reflects Judaism's universal concern:

Blessed are You, O Lord, our God, King of the universe, Who nourishes the entire world in His goodness—with grace, with kindness, and with mercy. He gives food to all flesh, for His kindness is eternal. And through His continual great goodness, we have not lacked [food], and may we never lack food, for the sake of His great name. For He is a benevolent God Who nourishes and sustains all, and is good to all, and prepares food for all of His creatures, whom He has created. As it is said: "You open Your hand and satisfy the desire of every living thing" (Psalms 145:16). Blessed are You, O Lord, Who provides food for all.

Paths of Peace

The world reflects the original intent of the Creator only when there is peace among all creatures (*Midrash: Bamidbar Rabbah* 21:1).

When the Messiah is revealed to Israel, the first thing he will do is establish peace. Thus, it is written: "How welcome upon the mountains are the feet of the messenger who announces peace" (Isaiah 52:7). (*Baraisa: Derech Eretz Zuta, Perek HaShalom*).

Rav Safra, after completing his formal prayers, used to say: "May it be Your will, O Lord, our God, to make peace among the Supernal Family and the Lower Family, as well as among the disciples who engage in [the study of] Your Torah . . ." (*Talmud: Berachos* 16b–17a).

Commentary: "The Supernal Family." The assembly of angels who preside over the nations of the world. When there is a dispute among the presiding angels in the supernal realm, there immediately ensues a dispute among the nations. Thus, [the angel told the Prophet Daniel], "And now I shall return to engage in battle with the angel of Persia" (Daniel 10:20). "The Lower Family." The assembly of the wise (Rashi, ad loc.).

"And Jacob said to them, 'My brothers, where are you from?'"
(Genesis 29:4). From here we learn that a person should always
include himself with others and address them as "brothers" and
"friends." He should hasten to greet them with greetings of peace.
Then the angels of peace and mercy will treat him in similar
fashion from above (*Midrash HaGadol* on *Bereshis* 29:4).

Great is peace, for with peace the Holy One, blessed be He,
will announce the Redemption of Israel, and with peace He will
console Jerusalem (*Midrash: Devarim Rabbah* 5:15).

See how beloved is peace: when the Holy One, blessed be He,
wished to bless Israel, He could not find a vessel great enough to
contain their blessings except for peace (*Midrash: Devarim Rabbah*
5:15).

See how great is the power of peace: the Holy One, blessed be
He, instructed [Israel] even to address their enemies first with
words of peace (*Midrash Tanchumah, Shoftim* 18).

"Seek peace and pursue it" (Psalms 34:15). That is, seek peace
in its place; pursue it when it is elsewhere (*Jerusalem Talmud:
Pe'ah* 1:1).

In the world's present state, it is permissible to flatter the
wicked for the sake of peace (*Midrash: Yalkut Shimoni, Vayishlach*
133).

The stones [of the Holy Temple] neither see nor hear, nor do they speak; but, since they make peace between Israel and their Father in Heaven, the Holy One, blessed be He, forbid striking them with iron implements. A person who makes peace between a husband and wife, one family and another, one city and another, one country and another, how much more should he be protected from all harm (*Baraisa: Toras Kohanim, Kedoshim* 20).

The purpose of the entire Torah is to establish peace, as it is written, "Her ways are ways of pleasantness, and all her paths are peace" (*Talmud: Gittin* 59b, citing Proverbs 3:17).

We must provide livelihood for the non-Jewish poor as well as for the Jewish poor; we must visit non-Jews when they are sick as well as our fellow Jews when they are sick; and we must attend to the burial of their dead as well as the burial of our own dead; for these are the ways of peace (*Talmud: Gittin* 61a).

Elijah the Prophet [the harbinger of the Messiah] will not come to distance people or to draw them closer, but to make peace between them (*Mishna: Eidiyus* 8:7).

Hillel used to say: Be of the disciples of Aaron—love peace and pursue peace, love all creatures and bring them near to the Torah (*Mishna: Avos* 1:12).

Midrash: If a person "loves peace and pursues peace" and restores peace, the Holy One, blessed be He, will grant him life in this world and in the World to Come (*Baraisa: Derech Eretz Zuta 9, Perek HaShalom*).

Commentary: The term "creatures" instead of "people" implies that Aaron would even reach out to individuals whose only redeeming virtue was the fact that God created them (Rabbi Menachem M. Schneerson, *Likkutei Sichos, Kedoshim* 5727 [1967]).

One who repudiates peace, repudiates the Divine name (*Zohar* III, *Bamidbar* 176b).

They might say, "Here is food, here is drink," but if there is no peace, all else is worthless. The verse states, "And I have given peace to the land" (Leviticus 26:6). This tells us that peace is equivalent to everything (*Baraisa: Toras Kohanim, Bechukosai* 1:1).

[The Torah forbids Jews to cultivate the land of Israel during the Sabbatical (seventh) Year.] It is permissible to encourage non-Jews [engaged in such labors] during the Sabbatical Year, but not Jews. Also, [it is proper to] offer them greetings in order to promote peace (*Talmud: Gittin* 61a).

Commentary: The Talmud explains that it is forbidden to actually assist them in their labors, but one may encourage them verbally. For instance, if one sees non-Jews at work in the fields, one may say to them, "May God give you strength," or, "May you be successful," etc., since they do not transgress in performing such labors. One may offer them greetings on their holidays, despite their association with idolatry. One may even greet them with God's name, as the rabbis state, for "Peace" (*Shalom*) is one of God's names (Rabbi Menachem Meiri, ad loc.).

A person should always seek peace with his brothers, relatives, and all men—including gentiles in the marketplace—in order that he may be beloved above, well-liked below, and acceptable to his fellow creatures. It was said of Rabbi Yochanan Ben Zakkai that no one ever preceded him in offering greetings of peace, even a non-Jew in the marketplace (*Talmud: Berachos* 17a).

Our Sages taught: One's mind should always be imbued with fear of God, his speech should be soft, turning away anger, and he should promote peace—with his father, his mother, his teacher, his comrade, and also with the non-Jew in the marketplace—that he may be beloved above and well-liked below. [Thus] he will be favorably received by all creatures, and all his days will be filled with good (*Midrash: Tanna D'vei Eliyahu Zuta* 1:1).

Concerning non-Jews, our Sages commanded us to visit their sick, to bury their dead, just as we bury the dead of the Jewish people, and to provide them with livelihood, just as we provide our fellow Jews with livelihood; for these are the ways of peace (*Gittin* 61a). Thus, the verse states: "God is good to all, and His mercies are upon all His works" (Psalms 145:9). And [of the Torah] it states: "Her ways are ways of pleasantness, and all her paths are of peace" (Proverbs 3:17). (Maimonides, *Mishneh Torah*, Laws of Kings 10:12).

Rabbi Yosef Saragossi, the teacher of Rabbi David Ben Zimra, was devoted to making peace between men, between husbands and wives, and even between non-Jews. [Therefore,] he merited that the soul of the Prophet Elijah appeared before him [to initiate him into the mysteries of the Torah] (Rabbi Elazar Azkari, *Sefer Chareidim* 8).

To the extent that there is peace in the world, mankind can be brought to serve God with one accord. Because of the peace that exists between people, they are able to enter into dialogue with one another and together think about the purpose of the world and its vanities. They can discuss the truth with one another—that ultimately nothing will remain of a person but the preparations he makes for the Eternal World. "Nothing accompanies a man—neither silver nor gold nor precious gems nor pearls—but only Torah and good deeds" (*Mishna: Avos* 6:9). By realizing this, each person will cast away his false gods of silver and turn to the Creator, His Torah, and Divine service; he will bring himself to the truth. However, when there is no peace, God forbid, or, worse, when there is actual strife, people cannot get together and discuss the ultimate purpose of life. Even when, on occasion, they do meet and talk to one another, [if someone speaks the truth] his words are not heard due to the climate of jealousy, conflict, spite, and disdain. Aggression and the desire to win arguments cannot bear the truth. Thus, the main thing that keeps most people far from the Creator is strife, which has become widespread because of our many sins. May God have mercy upon us (Rabbi Nachman of Breslov, *Likkutei Eitzos, Shalom* 4; also see *Likkutei Moharan* I:27).

"God is good for everything, and His mercies are upon all His works" (Psalms 145:9).

Commentary: "God is good for everything."[3] This alludes to prayer. A person who believes in God knows that He is "good for everything"—healing, sustenance, or whatever one needs. Therefore, he will direct his efforts primarily toward God (i.e., through prayer) and not be taken up with various strategies. One who doesn't believe in God, however, will pursue all sorts of mundane solutions to his problems. For example, if such a person becomes sick, he will pursue all sorts of medical treatments. The herbs required may not be available locally, or the local varieties may be of inferior quality. However, "God is good for everything." No matter from which ailment one needs to be healed, God is always available.

Prayer leads to universal peace. Thus, [the verse concludes,] "And His mercies are upon all His works." [When people turn to God as the ultimate power,] Divine mercy will be drawn forth to all creatures. [Consequently,] all creatures will have mercy upon one another, and there will be peace among them. As it is written, "And the wolf shall dwell with the lamb, and the leopard shall lie down with the kid. . . . They shall not harm or destroy" (Isaiah 11:6, 9), for there will be peace between them. Thus, "His mercies are upon all His works." [In other words, God will instill mercy in the hearts of all creatures, and they will treat each other accordingly.] As our Sages teach, "Whoever shows mercy to [God's] creatures is granted mercy from Heaven" (*Shabbos* 151b). [This is borne out by] the scriptural verse, "And [God] will give you mercy, and He will have mercy upon you" (Deuteronomy 13:18) (Rabbi Nachman of Breslov, *Likkutei Moharan* I, 14:11, abridged).

"Behold, for peace I had great bitterness . . ." (Isaiah 38:17). Just as all cures require bitter remedies, so does peace, which is

---

3. This is usually rendered, "God is good to all." However, Rabbi Nachman interprets the phrase as translated here.

a cure for everything. [As the Prophet Isaiah also states,] "Peace, peace to the far and near, says God, and I will heal him" (Isaiah 57:19) (Rabbi Nachman of Breslov, *Likkutei Moharan* I, 27:7).

On the subject of wars between nations and needless bloodshed, [Rabbi Nachman] said: "Many foolish beliefs that people once held, such as forms of idol-worship that demanded child-sacrifice, etc., have disappeared. But, as of yet, the foolish belief in the pursuit of war has not disappeared." He used to ridicule certain scientists, saying: "What great thinkers they must be, what ingenuity they must possess to invent amazing weapons that can kill thousands of people at once! Is there any greater foolishness than this—to murder so many people for nothing?" (*Chayei Moharan* 546).

Rabbi Nachman of Breslov predicted, "The Messiah will conquer the world without a shot being fired" (*Siach Sarfei Kodesh* II, 1:67).

The Patriarchs and Humanity

The Book of Genesis was called by the prophets the "Book of the Upright." The Talmud discusses this in *Avodah Zarah* 25a, citing two scriptural verses. It states in Joshua 10:13, "Is this not written in the Book of the Upright?" And it states in II Samuel 1:18, "To teach the children of Judah the use of the bow, as it is written in the Book of the Upright." Rabbi Yochanan explains: This refers to the book of Abraham, Isaac, and Jacob, who were called "upright," as the verse states, "Let my soul die the death of the upright" (Numbers 23:10). [However,] it needs to be understood why our Patriarchs are specifically termed "upright," and not righteous or devout, etc.

There is a verse from the Song of *Ha'azinu* ("Give ear, O heavens") that clarifies this issue: "The Rock, He is perfect in His deeds . . . righteous and upright is He" (Deuteronomy 32:4). The term "upright is He" vindicates the judgment by which the Holy One, blessed be He, destroyed the second Temple; for that was an obstinate and perverse generation. Although the people were righteous, devout, and dedicated to the study of Torah, they were not upright in their worldly doings. Therefore, because their hearts were full of causeless hatred for one another, they suspected anyone who did not act according to their own religious standards to be Sadducees or heretics. This led to widespread killing and to every sort of evil, until the Temple was destroyed. God's decree was just; the Holy One, blessed be He, is upright and does not tolerate righteous people like these. Rather, [God desires] those who act in an upright manner also in their

worldly doings, and not with crookedness, albeit for the sake of
Heaven. This [righteousness without compassion] caused the
destruction of the world and the ruin of civilization.

The Patriarchs were praiseworthy in that they were not only
righteous, devout, and lovers of God to the greatest possible
degree, but they were upright. That is, they related to the nations
of the world—even to the worst idolaters—with love and sought
their benefit, for this preserves creation. We see how our
Patriarch Abraham prostrated himself in prayer for the sake of
Sodom. Although he absolutely hated their wickedness and that
of their rulers, as his words to the King of Sodom clearly show, he
still sought their preservation. The Midrash states that the Holy
One, blessed be He, told Abraham: "'You love righteousness and
hate wickedness' (Psalms 45:8). You love to make My creatures
righteous and hate to see them remain wicked" (*Bereishis Rabba*,
Vayeirah, 49). Thus, he was truly a "father to a multitude of
nations" (Genesis 17:4). Even when a son does not follow the
straight path, [a father] nevertheless seeks his welfare and peace.
Similarly, Abraham spoke to Lot with amazing gentility and grace
(Genesis 13:8). We also see how easily Isaac was placated by his
enemies, for with a few words of appeasement from Avimelech
and his comrades, he was even more amiable than they had
anticipated (Genesis 26:28–30). Our Patriarch Jacob, after being
sorely vexed by Laban, knowing full well that [Laban] had sought
to destroy him, still spoke with him gently. About this the
Midrash declares, "The anger of the Patriarchs is superior to the
humility of the children" (*Bereishis Rabba*, *Vayeitzei*, 74). Moreover, [Jacob] was appeased immediately. There are many other
ways in which the Patriarchs exemplify how we should strive to
benefit the world. This is especially relevant to this book, the
Book of Genesis. [This name teaches us the great worth of
creation.] And, because of the Patriarchs, whose deeds [benefited
all humanity], it is also called the Book of the Upright (Rabbi
Naftali Zvi Berlin, *Ha'amek Davar*, Introduction to Genesis).

Good Citizenship

Rabbi Chananiah, deputy of the High Priest, said: Pray for the welfare of the government, for if not for the fear of it, people would eat one another alive (*Mishna: Avos* 3:2).

Commentary 1: This dictum is based on the verse: "And seek the peace of the city to which I have caused you to be exiled, and pray unto God on its behalf" (Jeremiah 29:7). Similarly, sacrifices on behalf of other nations were accepted and offered in the Holy Temple. This is another indication that the general welfare of all nations should be sought by Israel (Rashi, ad loc.).

Commentary 2: One should pray for the peace and welfare of the world and concern himself with the troubles and problems of all mankind (Rabbi Yonah of Gerona, ad loc.).

Commentary 3: The Mishna teaches us to pray for the welfare of the government. Based on this dictum, it has become customary in many Jewish communities to recite a blessing for the government during the Sabbath prayer service (*Tiferes Yisrael*, ad loc.).

Rabbi Yisrael [Salanter, founder of the modern Mussar movement,] used to pray for the welfare of the government. When he happened to be in a synagogue where the prayer was not read, he read it himself (Rabbi Chaim Ephraim Zaitchik, *Sparks of Mussar*).

37

The Talmud pledges the Jew to be loyal to the country of which he is a citizen, to love it as his homeland and to promote its welfare, as Jeremiah laid down at the time of the Babylonian captivity: "Build yourselves houses and dwell in them; plant gardens and eat their fruit; take yourselves wives and beget sons and daughters; take wives for your sons and give your daughters to husbands, that they may bear sons and daughters; multiply yourselves there and be not diminished. And seek the peace of the city where I have caused you to be exiled, and pray unto the Lord on its behalf; for in the peace thereof you shall have peace" (Jeremiah 29:5–7).

This has been the guiding principle of Jewish life always and everywhere. "The law of the land is the law" (*Gittin* 10b). In this concise statement, the Talmud lays down the norm for our behavior. It means that the law enacted by the government or state in which we live and whose subjects we are is binding upon us also from a religious point of view, and we must observe it (*Baba Kamma* 113a). In virtue of this principle, the Talmud, as we have seen, regards evasion of taxes and other dues as theft, even when they are levied only upon Jews (*Shulchan Aruch, Choshen Mishpat* 369:6). One must never overlook the respect due to the state (*Zevachim* 102a). One must pray for the welfare of the government, for were it not for fear of the government, society would disintegrate in a war of all against all (*Avos* 3:2). The prayer for the royal family and the government is part of our liturgy, and on seeing a non-Jewish king or queen, the Talmud enjoins us to recite a blessing: "Blessed are You, O Lord our God, King of the Universe, Who has given of Your glory to flesh and blood" (*Berachos* 58a).

We have already spoken of every Jew's obligation to deal honestly and truly with all people, Jews and non-Jews alike, even heathens and idolaters, and that any deviation from what is right and just in sale and purchase, weights and measures, counting and reckoning is an abomination to God.

That is not all. The Talmud also teaches that we have human and social obligations to all mankind—even to heathens and idolaters—to assist their poor, to attend their sick, to bury their dead, to support their aged, to respect their wise men, and to recite a special blessing on seeing an outstanding non-Jewish Sage (See *Gittin* 61a; *Kiddushin* 32b; *Berachos* 58a). This being the case with heathens and idolaters, how much more so does this apply to non-Jews who serve the God of the Torah, the Creator of heaven and earth; who keep the Seven Universal Laws of Noah, not to commit murder, not to steal, not to commit adultery, etc. In regard to the duties between man and man, the Talmud puts them on exactly the same level as Jews (Maimonides, *Mishneh Torah*, Laws of Kings 10:12). They have a claim to the benefit of all our religious duties, not only of justice but also of active brotherly love.

The masters of the Talmud may thus well be the only religious teachers who do not say, "Unless you believe as we do, you have no salvation." On the contrary, they teach that the righteous of all creeds have a share in the life of the World to Come (*Sanhedrin* 105a). The Talmud says that the laws of Moses were given to Israel to fulfill, but all other people are completely righteous before God if they scrupulously observe the Seven Universal Laws of Noah (Rabbi Samson Raphael Hirsch, *Judaism Eternal*, Chapter 5).

One must always seek the peace and well-being of society in order to preserve the covenant of civilization. Reason itself dictates that all members of society are bound to behave in ways that are mutually gratifying. Moreover, [since all members of society depend upon one other in order to survive and flourish,] one must appreciate the benefit one continually receives from others. The converse is also true: it is fitting to dislike and shun a thankless individual. Thus, our Sages taught, "There is no one so despised by the Holy One, blessed be He, as a thankless person."

This [dedication to the general welfare of society] conforms to reason in yet another way. There are great evil-doers in the world, and the harm and destruction that they bring about—through treachery, theft, embezzlement, murder, evil advice, dishonesty in business, etc.—is far worse than the harm that results from natural causes. When a person loves his fellow creatures and seeks their benefit, everyone seeks to remove these evils from him, for everyone is his friend and brother. But one who bears no love for humanity in his heart evokes little sympathy from others. As our Sages taught, "Hatred of mankind drives a person out of the world" (*Avos* 2:11) (Rabbi Pinchas Eliyahu of Vilna, *Sefer HaBris* II, 13:3).

Honesty in Business[4]

"Righteousness, righteousness shall you pursue" (Deuteronomy 16:20). Why does the Torah repeat the word "righteousness"? Because righteousness must be pursued both in our relationship with Jews and in our relationship with non-Jews, even with those who worship idols (Rabbeinu Bachaye, *Kad HaKemach, Gezeilah*).

A Jew who steals from a non-Jew must make full restitution. Stealing from a non-Jew is even worse than stealing from a fellow Jew because it profanes God's name. If one steals from a non-Jew and subsequently denies it and dies, his death does not atone for him, for he has profaned God's name (*Tosefta* on *Baba Kamma* 10:8; also note *B. Kamma* 113b).

---

4. The reader may wonder at the amount of material included on this and related subjects. There are several reasons for this. It should be noted that each selection highlights a different facet of this prohibition. Also, the lengthy discussion of such matters in rabbinic literature deserves more than summary mention. There is yet another factor that is easily overlooked by the modern reader, accustomed to the ethnic homogeneity of an open society. Historically, the Jews have lived in relatively insular communities (by their own choice as well as by anti-Semitic decree); their main interaction with non-Jews was in the marketplace. Therefore, the issue of honesty in business was of greater concern to the rabbis than other forms of abuse or oppression, which were less likely to occur. Finally, it must be said that one of the common attacks of anti-Semitic propaganda is that the Jewish religion sanctions the economic exploitation of non-Jews, a claim that rabbinic literature clearly refutes.

Now that the exile has been prolonged beyond its time, the people of Israel must remove themselves from worldly vanities and take hold of "the seal of the Holy One, blessed be He" (*Shabbos* 55a), which is truth, and never speak falsehood— neither to Jews or non-Jews, nor deceive them in any manner. Rather, they should "sanctify themselves in what is permissible to them," as it states: "The remnant of Israel shall do no wrong" (Zephaniah 3:13); they should neither speak deceitfully, nor should their tongues utter trickery. And when the Holy One, blessed be He, comes to redeem them, the nations of the world will testify at the judgment, "Do so—for they are true, and the Torah of Truth is in their mouths." However, if they behave dishonestly, [the nations] will say, "See what the Holy One, blessed be He, has done: He has chosen for His portion thieves and tricksters" (Rabbi Moshe of Coucy, *Sefer Mitzvos Gadol*, Positive Commandment 74).

Stealing from a non-Jew is even worse than stealing from a Jew, for [aside from its intrinsic evil] it may lead to greater harm. The non-Jewish victim may feel justified in later avenging himself upon another, innocent Jew. Also, the rest of the local Jewish community may suffer in reprisal for the actions of this one sinner (Rabbi Yehudah HeChasid, *Sefer Chasidim* 600, with commentaries ad loc.).

It is forbidden to speak false words of flattery. Rather, one's words should come from the heart. Causing another person to mistake one's true feelings or intentions is also a form of theft and is forbidden, whether the other is a Jew or non-Jew. Those who disparage non-Jews [in the jargon spoken by Jews] while offering them greetings, giving the impression that their words are kind, are sinners. Indeed, there is no greater emotional deception than this. However, one may hasten to greet non-Jewish dignitaries, even if one knows them to be wicked, for the sake of peace (ibid., 51).

I write this for future generations: I have seen many people become wealthy by causing non-Jews to err in business in order to gain profit thereby. However, they did not remain successful. In the end, all their wealth was confiscated by the government, and their descendants were left without an inheritance (Rabbi Moshe Rivkah's, *Be'er HaGolah* on *Shulchan Aruch, Choshen Mishpat, Hil. Geneivah* 348).

Whoever steals even the least amount transgresses the scriptural commandment not to steal and must make full restitution. This applies whether one steals the money of a Jew or a non-Jew, an adult or a child (Rabbi Yosef Karo, *Shulchan Aruch, Choshen Mishpat* 348:2; note *Be'er Heitev*, ad loc., citing numerous rabbinic authorities of the same opinion; also, see *Chasam Sofer, Choshen Mishpat, Teshuvah* 185).

If [a Jew] has borrowed an object from a non-Jew, it is forbidden [for the Jew] to deny it, for this constitutes actual theft. Moreover, even if one purchases an object from a non-Jew, it is forbidden to trick him; as it is written, "And he shall reckon with his purchaser" (Leviticus 25:50), which refers to a non-Jew. One must sell the merchandise for the price mutually agreed upon. [A Jew] who deceives [a non-Jewish buyer] in a financial transaction is tantamount to a robber. Even to deceive [a non-Jew] about the nature of a purchase without any financial loss is forbidden (Rabbi Shlomo Ganzfried, *Kitzur Shulchan Aruch* 182:4).

It is forbidden to buy stolen goods from a thief or a robber. It makes no difference whether he is a Jew or a non-Jew; for the non-Jew, too, is forbidden to rob or steal, even from another non-Jew. [The prohibition of theft] is one of the Seven Laws [of Noah]. To purchase stolen goods is a serious transgression, since this aids and abets evil-doers. Concerning this it is written, "Whoever divides with a thief hates his own soul" (Proverbs 29:24), for if the thief found no buyers he would not steal. However, one may do so in order to restore stolen goods to the rightful owners (Rabbi Shlomo Ganzfried, *Kitzur Shulchan Aruch* 182:8).

It is forbidden by Jewish law to steal or embezzle anything at all—whether something of great or little value, whether from a Jew or a non-Jew, even if the non-Jew has afflicted the Jew. Stealing from a non-Jew is even worse than stealing from a Jew, since [the victim] will surely not forgive him. Also, his transgression will cause the angel who oversees the nation of the non-Jewish victim to steal the Heavenly blessings that are conferred upon the Jewish people from Above, measure for measure. This subject touches upon extremely deep matters; therefore, one should be most careful [not to violate this prohibition] (*Ben Ish Chai, Halachos* I, *Ki Seitzei* 7).

Even if [a Jew] sells a non-Jew a measure that is lacking to the slightest degree, he violates a scriptural prohibition and must restore [what he owes], for he deceived [the non-Jew] and thus is an actual thief. This act falls within the category of [the verse], "Whoever does such things is an abomination unto the Lord, your God; whoever commits any wrong" (Deuteronomy 25:16).

Our rabbis state that this includes wronging a non-Jew (*Baba Basra* 88b) (*Ben Ish Chai, Halachos* I, *Ki Seitzei* 6).

If a non-Jew who observes the Seven Laws of Noah makes an error to his detriment in a business transaction, one must not take advantage of this mistake, for to do so is strictly forbidden. Also, one must never belittle him; on the contrary, he deserves a greater measure of respect than the Jew who neglects the study of Torah (Rabbi Yehudah HeChasid, *Sefer Chasidim* 358).

[Not only does a Jew sin by permitting himself to wrong a non-Jew, but] one who steals from a non-Jew will eventually steal from other Jews, as well (*Midrash: Tanna D'vei Eliyahu Rabba* 28:5).

Turn away, turn away, go out from there—touch no unclean thing! Go out from its midst; be clean, you who bear the vessels of the Lord (Isaiah 52:11).

Commentary: This verse underscores the duty of every Jew to be the strictest judge of his own conduct. He can never offer the excuse to God that others are no better in their dealings between man and man, in the exercise of honesty, integrity, and compassion. Being a Jew demands a higher, not a lower, degree of conscientiousness in such matters. Even keeping within the strict limits of the law is not enough. Honest actions must be the result of noble and "clean" feelings. The Jew must never forget that he is a *kohen* (priest) to mankind, a "bearer of the vessels of the Lord." These vessels are the precepts he follows, the teachings with which he should be permeated. Were his life not in harmony with the Torah's commandments, were he less than impeccably honest and straightforward in dealing with his Jewish and non-Jewish brothers, demonstrating the love of one's neighbor that the Torah advocates, he would indeed dishonor the "vessels of the Lord" with which he has been entrusted. The tools meant to bring mankind back to God would be rendered useless. Thus, Judaism teaches that any act of dishonesty toward a non-Jew is more grievous before God than if it had been practiced against a Jew (Rabbi Mendel Hirsch, ad loc.).

Elijah's Rebuke

The Prophet Elijah taught: A fellow came and set beside me, who was familiar with Scripture but not Mishna. He said to me, "Master, it once happened that I sold a non-Jew four *curs* of dates, which I weighed in a dark booth by approximation. [The non-Jew] told me, 'You and the Lord in Heaven know what you have measured out for me.' My measure lacked three *s'in* of dates. I received the money and purchased a flask of oil, which I put in the place where I had sold the dates to the non-Jew. [However,] the flask tore, and the oil spilled out."

[The Prophet Elijah] told [the shopkeeper], "My son, the verse states, 'You shall not oppress your neighbor, nor shall you steal' (Leviticus 19:13). Your brother is like your neighbor, and your neighbor is like your brother. Have you not learned that stealing from a non-Jew is forbidden—and, needless to say, stealing from your brother? Thus, when the Holy One, blessed be He, saw that people were oppressing one another by robbing and stealing, He reiterated through the Prophet Ezekiel, 'His father, because he cruelly oppressed, robbed the loot of a brother and did wrong among his people—behold, he died for his sin'" (Ezekiel 18:18) (*Midrash: Tanna D'vei Eliyahu Rabba* 15:7).

Measure for Measure

Once there was a Jewish man whose sons and daughter died as soon as they were married. He sought the advice of a Torah Sage, to whom he explained: "I had a non-Jewish neighbor who died. Soon afterward, my children died, and the money I had given them was inherited by their wives and husbands. If Heaven judged that I was unworthy of having descendants, why didn't my children die before marriage, so that at least my wealth would not have gone [to strangers]?" He concluded, "As long as that non-Jew was alive, everything was fine."

The Sage said: "Perhaps your wealth was acquired dishonestly."

The man replied: "I never wronged anyone—except that non-Jew, whom I used to deceive in business."

"When he died, his angel told him the truth," the Sage explained, "and he cried out in anguish. The Holy One, blessed be He, takes up the cause of the oppressed, whether they are Jews or non-Jews. [Therefore, Heaven decreed that you be punished for oppressing this man and his family, measure for measure]" (Rabbi Yehudah HeChasid, *Sefer Chasidim* 661).

Fairness Toward One's Employees

Never overwork an employee, whether he is a Jew or a non-Jew. Such practices lead to a person's downfall: either he or his children will be reduced to poverty. For example, if one hires a tradesman to do some work or a teacher for one's children, do not burden him excessively or make demands beyond the original terms of agreement. An employer should never stipulate that a worker produce more than he can. If one knows that a worker can only walk a certain number of miles, he should not say, "I am hiring you, provided that you walk such-and-such a distance," knowing that this is beyond the man's ability. Even if a worker agrees, it is forbidden to impose a task upon him that he cannot accomplish or a burden that he cannot bear (Rabbi Yehudah HeChasid, *Sefer Chasidim* 1074).

A Master of Accounts

[Rabbi Yisrael Meir HaKohen, also known as the Chofetz Chaim,] was careful not to cheat his non-Jewish as well as his Jewish customers. One market day a non-Jewish customer left a herring in Rabbi Yisrael Meir's store. Rabbi Yisrael Meir made every effort to find out who the man was, but to no avail. The next market day, he distributed free herring to all his non-Jewish customers (Rabbi Chaim Ephraim Zaitchik, *Sparks of Mussar*).

Another time, a peasant woman bought salt in his store and left some behind. In order to make restitution, Rabbi Yisrael Meir took a whole sack of salt over to the village and distributed it (ibid.).

A cow was kept in Rabbi Yisrael Meir's house to provide milk, and here again Rabbi Yisrael Meir was careful in all the laws of damages. He chose a cow that was known not to do harm, and he himself guarded it from causing damage. At night when the cow came in from the pasture, he would check that the door was closed so that the cow could not get out. In the morning he would warn the herdsman not to let the cow tread on or graze in other people's fields.

Once Rabbi Yisrael Meir set out on a journey and forgot to instruct his family to watch the cow carefully, so he sent a special messenger to admonish them about it.

While Rabbi Yisrael Meir was in a nearby town, he asked some wagoners headed for Radin to deliver an urgent message to his wife. The wagoners, curious about what was so urgent, opened the letter. To their great surprise, they read a warning not to let the cow walk through the streets on market day. On that day many wagons of non-Jews would drive through town, and Rabbi Yisrael was worried that the cow might take some hay from them (ibid.).

One Standard

The Talmud Yerushalmi (*Baba Metzia* 2:5) tells the story of Shimon ben Shetach, who worked in the flax business and struggled to make a living. His disciples advised him to give up his business and buy a donkey, which would provide a better source of income. Shimon ben Shetach agreed, and his students bought a donkey from an Arab pagan. After buying the animal, these disciples found a large diamond tied to it, and they brought both the animal and the jewel to their teacher. Upon seeing the acquisitions of his students, Shimon ben Shetach asked, "Did the Arab know that there was a diamond tied to the donkey?" The disciples said, "No." At that point, Shimon ben Shetach said to his disciples, "Go immediately and return the diamond." The disciples, however, were curious—is it not stated that all agree that the lost goods of a pagan are permitted to be retained? Shimon ben Shetach responded, "Do you think that I am such a barbarian? I am more interested in hearing the exclamation, 'Blessed be the God of the Jews' from the mouths of pagans than I am in making a living." Although perhaps the act of keeping the diamond might not have been stealing according to the law, it was forbidden as an act of "barbarism," since "the remnant of Israel shall not do iniquity or speak lies" (*Zephaniah* 3:13). It is inconsistent with *k'vod habriyos* (the dignity of all creatures) and human rights.

In this story, Shimon ben Shetach gives a remarkable definition of the term "barbarian." According to him, anyone who fails to apply a uniform standard of *mishpat* (justice) and *tzedek* (righ-teousness) to all human beings, regardless of origin, color, or creed is deemed barbaric (Rabbi Ahron Soloveitchik, *Logic of the Heart, Logic of the Mind,* "Civil Rights and the Dignity of Man").

Cosmic Justice

[Based on the biblical example of Noah] it is said: "Merit is given to the meritorious, and guilt to those who are guilty." [Noah lived in a righteous manner, therefore the world was renewed through him. Similarly, Divine Providence gives people the opportunity to be agents of good or evil based upon their previous actions.] This rule applies to all the families of the earth, Jews and non-Jews alike (*Midrash: Tanna D'vei Eliyahu Rabba* 16:1).

If a person renounces the evil of his ancestors, he shall be deemed righteous and receive Divine beneficence. If a person does not renounce the evil of his ancestors, he, too, is punished. This rule applies to all the families of the earth, Jews and non-Jews alike (ibid., 17:19).

The Holy One, blessed be He, repays each person according to his deeds, measure for measure[5] (*Talmud: Sanhedrin* 90a).

---

5. Also note the Mishna's teaching in *Sotah* 1:7 and *Avos* 2:6 that God causes whatever happens to a person to reflect his or her own deeds.

Righteous Non-Jews

In the ultimate future, the Holy One, blessed be He, will grant
life in the World to Come to righteous non-Jews, as it is written,
"Your *kohanim* (priests) will be garbed in righteousness" (Psalms
132:9). This refers to the righteous gentiles, who are *kohanim* to
the Holy One, blessed be He (*Midrash: Yalkut*, II Kings 296).

"Your *kohanim* (priests) will be garbed in righteousness, and
your pious ones will exult in song" (Psalms 132:9). "Your
kohanim" refers to righteous non-Jews, such as Antoninus and his
comrades, who are the *kohanim* (priests) of the Holy One, blessed
be He, in this world. "Your pious ones" refers to the transgressors
of Israel [when their repentance has been accepted by God]
(*Midrash: Tanna D'vei Eliyahu Zuta* 20:6).

Righteous gentiles have a portion in the World to Come
(*Tosephta, Sanhedrin* 13:1; Maimonides, *Mishneh Torah*, Laws of
Repentance 3:5; ibid., Laws of Testimony 11:10).

[The Holy One, blessed be He, declares:] Every non-Jew who
says, "There is no other God," I will restore to life in the World
to Come (*Midrash: Pirkei D'Rabbi Eliezer* 34).

✑

The Holy One, blessed be He, does not withhold reward from non-Jews who perform His commandments (*Jerusalem Talmud: Pe'ah* 1:1).

✑

"He will judge the nations with uprightness" (Psalms 9:9). When the Holy One, blessed be He, judges the nations of the world, He will recall the merit of the upright ones among them (*Midrash: Yalkut*, Psalms 643).

✑

There is a place in the Garden of Eden reserved for pious individuals of all nations (*Zohar, Pekudei*).

✑

"The wicked shall go to the abyss and all the nations who forget God" (Psalms 9:18). Rabbi Yehoshua said: The verse does not simply state, "all the nations." Thus, it teaches that only those idolatrous nations who forget God [will be punished, not those who believe in God] (*Midrash Shochar Tov*, Psalm 9).

✑

The prophet Bilaam will not enter the World to Come, however, other non-Jews will. According to whom is this statement? Rabbi Yehoshua.

[It is written:] "The wicked shall go to the abyss, all the nations who forget the Lord" (Psalms 9:18). Rabbi Eliezer [gave the following interpretation]: "The wicked shall go to the abyss"— these are the sinners of Israel. "All the nations who forget

God"—these are the sinful nations of the world. This is the opinion of Rabbi Eliezer.

Rabbi Yehoshua declared, "The verse refers to all the nations; for does it not say 'all the nations who forget God' [without distinction]? Rather, interpret it as follows: 'The wicked shall go to the abyss'—who are they?—'all the nations who forget God.'" [However, both Jews and non-Jews who remember God have a place in the World to Come] (*Talmud: Sanhedrin* 105a; *Rashi,* ad loc.).

Every non-Jew who strives to observe the Seven Commandments of Noah is considered one of the righteous of the nations. He or she is reckoned among the faithful and possesses a portion in the World to Come (Rabbi Menachem Meiri on *Sanhedrin* 57a).

"Come, let us descend and confuse their speech" (Genesis 11:7). [God] confused their tongues, so that they could not understand the language of one another. The original language was Hebrew, with which the world was created. The Holy One, blessed be He, declared: "In this world, because of the Evil Inclination, My creatures have become divided into seventy languages. However, in the World to Come, they shall all become one, that they may call upon My name and worship Me." As the verse states, "For then I shall convert the nations to a pure speech, that all of them may call upon the name of God, to serve Him with a common accord" (Zephaniah 3:9). (*Midrash Tanchuma, Noah* 19).

"Conceal them in the refuge of Your Presence from the bands of the wicked; hide them as a treasure in a shelter (*sukkah*) from quarrelsome tongues" (Psalms 31:21).

According to the author of _Sh'vilei Emunah_, this includes even those non-Jews who do not properly keep all Seven Universal Laws of Noah but are friendly to the Jewish people and treat them with kindness. [After death] they sit outside [the gates of Paradise], from whence they are taken away to be judged, together with other sinners—those who are called "quarrelsome tongues." However, they are saved (Rabbi Moshe Teitelbaum of Ujheli, _Yismach Moshe, Tetzaveh_ 183b).

Judaism does not say, "There is no salvation outside of me." Although disparaged because of its alleged particularism, the Jewish religion actually teaches that the upright of all peoples are headed toward the highest goal. Of all men, it is the rabbis who point to the predictions of the prophets and singers of a new day for humanity and emphasize that there is no mention of Priests, Levites, and Israelites, but that only the just, honest, and upright of all peoples are included in the noblest blessings (Rabbi Samson Raphael Hirsch, _Judaism Eternal_, chap. 5).

The Crown of Torah

There are three crowns: the crown of Torah, the crown of the priesthood, and the crown of kingship. The crown of the priesthood was claimed by Aharon. (Aharon was the first *Kohen Gadol* (High Priest), from whom all other *kohanim* (priests) descend.) The crown of kingship was claimed by David.[6] The crown of Torah was made available to everyone in the world. Whoever earns it, I will consider as if I had made available the three crowns, and he had been worthy of them all (*Baraisa: Sifri, Korach* 46).

A non-Jew who engages in the study of Torah is comparable to the *Kohen Gadol* (High Priest) (*Talmud: Avodah Zara* 3a).

How do we know that even a non-Jew who studies Torah is comparable to the *Kohen Gadol* (High Priest)? It is written, "If a person does them, he shall live by them" (Leviticus 18:5). The verse does not speak of "Priests, Levites, and Israelites," but "a person." From this we understand that even a non-Jew who studies Torah is comparable to the *Kohen Gadol* (*Talmud: Baba Kamma* 38a).

---

6. King David, from whom the Messiah and all Jewish kings descend, established the first Jewish commonwealth, with Jerusalem as its capitol.

Commentary: If a person casts off the yoke of the Torah and religious observance, although he may still perform a few commandments gratuitously, he no longer receives the same reward as one who was commanded and obeyed. He is merely like one who performs a good deed of his own volition. Nevertheless, the Holy One, blessed be He, does not withhold the reward of anyone who labors in the study of Torah for the sake of Heaven. Thus, it explicitly states concerning a non-Jew who studies Torah—although he only studies the Seven Commandments of Noah, and although in general [the rest of] his nation may transgress them—that since he fulfills them as God's commandments, he is comparable to the *Kohen Gadol* (High Priest). Even for the performance of other commandments, the Holy One, blessed be He, does not withhold recompense. This even applies to a pleasant word or for alacrity in performing a religious precept, albeit one that is not time-bound [and hence requires alacrity]. It is a basic rule in the performance of God's commandments that a person is rewarded according to his deeds (Rabbi Menachem Meiri, ad loc.).

The Holy One, blessed be He, declared: There is no oil like Torah, and no oil like good deeds, as the verse states, "Your ointments are fragrant, for your flowing oils you are renowned; therefore, do the maidens (*alamos*) love you" (Song of Songs 1:3). If the non-Jewish nations were to discern with wisdom, understanding, knowledge, and intellect and apprehend the substance of your Torah, they would love you wholeheartedly, whether it was good for them or bad for them. Thus, the verse concludes, "Therefore, do the maidens (*alamos*) love you"[7] (*Midrash: Tanna D'vei Eliyahu Rabba* 6:17).

---

7. The Hebrew word *alamos* is similar to the word *olam*, i.e., the world. However, the interpretation of the Midrash, "If the non-Jewish nations were to discern . . ." is conditional, whereas the scriptural verse itself seems to be stating a fact. A possible explanation is that the verse alludes to the revelations

A non-Jew who accepts the Seven Universal Laws of Noah and diligently observes them is one of the pious of the nations. He has a share in the World to Come—provided that he accepts them and performs them because the Holy One, blessed be He, commanded them in the Torah and made known through Moses, our teacher, that they had been enjoined upon the descendants of Noah in former times. However, if he observes them as a result of his own reason, he is not deemed a resident alien or one of the pious of the nations, but one of their Sages (Maimonides, *Mishneh Torah*, Laws of Kings 8:11, Yemenite manuscript version).

The Almighty expressly commanded Moses, our teacher, to influence the entire world to accept the Seven Universal Laws of Noah. All who accept these Seven Universal Laws and diligently fulfill them are deemed righteous gentiles who merit a portion in the World to Come (ibid., 8:10–11).

If a non-Jew who has accepted upon himself the Seven Universal Laws of Noah wishes to perform one of the Torah's other commandments in order to receive a Divine reward, he should not be deterred from properly doing so. If he brings a voluntary sacrifice [to the Holy Temple in Jerusalem], it is accepted from him. If he gives charity, it is accepted from him (ibid., 10:10).

of Godliness that will characterize the Messianic era. Then the enmity of the nations toward Israel will be turned to love.

If two non-Jews wish to present a dispute before a Jewish court for adjudication [and both parties agree to abide by the final verdict], their case is accepted (ibid., 10:12).

If Christians observe the Seven Universal Laws of Noah, as they are commanded, not only are they undeserving of any denigration in the least, but they undoubtedly merit praise. Thus our Sages have taught: "The pious of the nations have a share in the World to Come" (Rabbi Yaacov Emden, *Sefer Shimush* 24a).

All those who believe in the Torah of Moses, be they from whatever nation, are not in the category of idol-worshipers and the like, even though they do not fully observe it; for they are not commanded to do so (Rabbi Yaacov Emden, *Siddur*, Volume II).

From which scriptural source do we learn that when even one person sits and occupies himself with the Torah, the Holy One, blessed be He, rewards him? From the verse: "He sits alone [and studies] in stillness; he takes [the reward] unto himself" (Lamentations 3:28). (*Mishna: Avos* 3:2).

Commentary: This verse cited by the Mishna is from the prophetic book that laments the destruction of the Holy Temple. The fact that a Jew must sit alone and study Torah is itself a sign of the exile. For concerning the Era of the Redemption, it is written: "The occupation of the entire world will be solely to know God" (*Mishneh Torah, Laws of Kings* 12:5). (Rabbi Menachem Mendel Schneerson of Lubavitch, *Sichos Shabbos, Devarim* 5741).

The Righteous Proselyte

And the children of the foreigner who join themselves to God, to minister unto Him and to love His name, to be His servants—everyone who observes the Sabbath, not to profane it, and all who uphold My covenant—I will bring them to My holy mountain and cause them to rejoice in My house of prayer; their burnt offerings and sacrifices will be favored upon My altar; for My House shall be called a house of prayer for all the nations. Thus says the Lord, God, who gathers the dispersed of Israel: I shall gather still more to those already gathered (Isaiah 56:6–8).

Commentary: "A house of prayer for all the nations." Not only for [native-born] Israelites but also for converts. "I shall gather still more." Non-Jews who are destined to convert and attach themselves to Israel. "To those already gathered." In addition to those gathered of Israel (Rashi, ad loc.).

The Jewish people went into exile for the sake of those destined to convert (*Talmud: Pesachim* 87b).

"And if a stranger (*ger*) dwells with you in your land, you shall do him no wrong. As the native-born among you shall be the stranger who dwells with you; and you shall love him as yourselves, for you were strangers in the land of Egypt" (Leviticus

19:33–34; the Hebrew word *ger* means both stranger and proselyte). Do not say to the proselyte, "Yesterday you worshiped idols, and now you have come under the wings of the *Shechina* (Divine Presence)" (*Baraisa: Toras Kohanim* 8:2).

Rabbi Shimon Ben Lakish said: Whoever wrongs a convert is as if he wrongs God (*Talmud: Chagiga* 5a).

Rabbi Shimon Bar Yochai said: We read, "But those who love Him are as the sun when it goes forth in its might" (Judges 5:31). Now, who is greater, one who loves the king or one whom the king loves? You must say: one whom the king loves. And the verse attests, "And He loves the stranger" (Deuteronomy 10:18). (*Baraisa: Mechilta* 18).

There is a special place in the Garden of Eden for converts (*Zohar Chadash, Lech Lecha* 26a).

The souls of converts come from beneath the wings of the *Shechina* (Divine Presence) (*Zohar I, Hakdamah* 13a).

In the future world, the righteous converts are destined to become *kohanim* (priests) (*Midrash: Shemos Rabba* 19).

When the Jewish people heed the will of God, a [spirit of holiness] passes through the world. When [this spirit] finds a certain righteous non-Jew, it causes him to come forth and cleave to the Jewish people (*Jerusalem Talmud: Berachos* 2:8).

Whenever the Torah speaks of righteous Israelites, it includes among them the righteous converts (*Talmud: Megilla* 17b).

When a non-Jew comes to convert, he or she is asked: "Why do you wish to convert? Don't you know that the Jews are now afflicted, oppressed, down-trodden, and torn, and sufferings are visited upon them?" If the prospective convert answers: "I know, and I am unworthy [of joining them]," he or she is accepted immediately and taught several simple precepts, as well as several difficult precepts (*Talmud: Yevamos* 47a).

"Those who dwell in His shadow shall be revived" (Hosea 14:8). Rabbi Abbahu taught: These are the converts who take refuge in the shadow of the Holy One, blessed be He. "Their remembrance will be like the wine of Lebanon" (ibid., 14:7). The Holy One, blessed be He, declares: the names of converts are as precious to Me as the wine libation offered on the altar. Why is the Holy Temple called "Lebanon"? Because Scripture alludes to it as "this goodly mountain and the Lebanon" (Deuteronomy 3:25). Rabbi Shimon Bar Yochai taught: Why is it called "Lebanon"? Because it rendered the transgressions of Israel white (*lavan*) as snow (Midrash: *Vayikra Rabba* 1:2).

Just as all streams flow to the sea, all converts are gathered unto Israel (*Midrash: Koheles Rabbasi* 1:18).

Why was the Torah given in the desert? Just as a desert is ownerless and available to all, so are the words of Torah ownerless and available to anyone who wishes to learn. No one can say, "I am a Torah scholar, and the Torah belongs to me and my ancestors—you and your ancestors are not Torah scholars but converts." [The Torah is called] "an inheritance of the congregation of Jacob" (Deuteronomy 33:4). Thus, whoever joins the congregation of Jacob and engages in Torah study is equal to the High Priest (*Kohen Gadol*) (*Midrash Tanchuma, Vayakhel* 8).

The Talmud states that before God gave the Torah at Mount Sinai, He offered it to all the other nations of the world. Each one rejected it, except for the Children of Israel (*Avodah Zarah* 2b). However, there were certain individuals who did wish to accept the Torah. These souls were destined to become righteous converts. Likewise, there were certain Israelites who refused. These souls were destined to become apostates[8] (Rabbi Yisrael Meir HaKohen, the "Chofetz Chaim," cited by Rabbi Elchanan Wasserman in *Chayei HaMussar*, vol. II, pp. 157–158).

"And you shall love the convert" (Deuteronomy 10:19). The Torah commands us to love anyone who enters under the wings of the Divine Presence, having fully accepted the Torah and its

---

8. This is ascribed to the Ger Tzedek of Vilna in Rabbi Meir Yashar's *Chofetz Chaim U'Pa'alo*, pp. 292–293. The same teaching appears in Rabbi Yaakov Prager's *Tovas Yaakov, Yisro*, in the name of Rabbi Akiva Eiger. In a related vein, the Maharsha on *Shabbos* 146a states that when the Torah was given to the Jewish People at Mt. Sinai, the *mazal* (destiny) of the future convert was also present. I am grateful to Rabbi Yehoshua Leiman for the primary source reference and to Rabbi Yaakov Weiss for these additional ones.

precepts. In thirty-six verses the Torah urges us to love the convert and not to wrong him in any way, either monetarily or verbally, for converts are more beloved by God and are more precious to Him than Israel. This may be compared to two people, one who loves the king and the other who is loved by the king. Which is greater? The one who is loved by the king. Israel loves the Holy One, blessed be He, whereas the Holy One, blessed be He, loves the convert. As the verse states, "He loves the convert, granting him food and clothing" (Deuteronomy 10:18). Therefore, it is incumbent upon us to love the one whom the King loves (Rabbi Yehudah HeChasid, *Sefer Chasidim* 116).

If a good-hearted Jew marries a convert who is [similarly] kind, modest, benevolent, and pleasant toward others, their children will be righteous and virtuous. Indeed, it is better to marry the child of such parents than to marry the offspring of those who are born Jewish but do not possess these fine qualities[9] (Rabbi Yehudah HeChasid, *Sefer Chasidim* 377).

These are the descendants of converts: masters of Scripture, masters of Mishna, masters of commerce, Sages, and men of skill; their seed shall endure forever (*Midrash: Bamidbar Rabba* 8:9).

When the idolatrous priest Jethro decided to serve God and declared, "Now I know that God is greater than all powers," the Divine name was glorified and exalted from every aspect (*Zohar* II, *Yisro*, 69a, citing Exodus 18:11).

---

9. See *Horayos* 13a.

Through converts and penitents, the Oneness of God is revealed through the very multiplicity of creation. Since they, too, come forth in order to become incorporated into His absolute Oneness, this is most precious to God. Therefore, the Torah stresses that one should love and encourage the proselyte. Similarly, our Sages greatly praised the spiritual levels attained by penitents, who, after having distanced themselves, strive to return to God (Rabbi Nosson Sternhartz, *Likkutei Halachos, P'rika U'te'ina,* 4:3).

"Peace, peace, to the far and the near" (Isaiah 57:19). Converts and penitents often feel the pain of their distance from holiness, due to their past sins and the extent to which they have not yet purified their bodies. Nevertheless, they must also realize how close they really are to God—just as they are right now—for God's love and mercy is limitless. When they grasp this, they can truly draw close to God. These two seemingly opposite perceptions are implied by the verse, "Peace, peace to the far and the near."

This principle is also reflected by the tradition that when a non-Jew comes to convert, he is initially discouraged. This is a consequence of his distance from holiness. However, the entire purpose of this initial discouragement is to strengthen his resolve and to draw him closer. For if after everything, he says, "I know that I am unworthy," that is, he recognizes his distance from holiness, then he is immediately accepted (Rabbi Nosson Sternhartz, *Likkutei Halachos, Shilu'ach HaKan* 5:17).

"And Jethro, the priest of Midian, father-in-law of Moses, heard of all that God had done for Moses and for Israel, his people . . ." (Exodus 18:1). Because he was the father-in-law of Moses, he heard and converted. For everything Moses worked to accomplish, during his life and now, after his death, was only to make converts [and bring all of humanity back to God] (Rabbi Nachman of Breslov, *Likkutei Moharan* I:215; concerning the difficulties of this task, note ibid., I:59, 228).

Rabbi Shimon Ben Lakish states: The convert who accepts the Torah due to his own conviction is higher than the thousands of Israelites who stood at Mount Sinai and accepted the Torah amidst thunder and lightning (*Midrash Tanchuma, Lech Lecha* 6, on Genesis 14:1).

Ben Hay Hay used to say: Commensurate with the effort is the reward (*Mishna: Avos* 5:23).

Commentary: The rabbis explain that Ben Hay Hay was a convert (Tosefos, *Chagiga* 9b). This is reflected in his teaching. It is a principle of our faith that God rewards men for observing His commandments (Maimonides, *Commentary on the Mishna, Sanhedrin*, intro. to chap. 10, Principle 11). This Mishna teaches that in calculating that reward, God looks not only at the task accomplished, but also at the effort invested. When a person struggles to fulfill a commandment, God increases his reward.

This particularly applies to the effort one invests in a commandment when he is not obligated to do so—to perform a commandment in a beautiful and conscientious manner or to engage in a positive action beyond the letter of the law. Perhaps the most complete expression of this concept is the act of conversion. A non-Jew is not at all required to accept the burden of Judaism; indeed, he should initially be discouraged from doing so (*Yevamos* 47a). Therefore, the painstaking effort the convert expends in the observance of the commandments surely deserves a great reward (Rabbi Menachem M. Schneerson of Lubavitch, *Likkutei Sichos*, vol. 27, p. 387).

The Sages and the High Priest

A certain High Priest (*Kohen Gadol*) once left the Holy Temple, followed by the entire assembly. However, when the people saw Shemayah and Avtalyon,[10] they left [the High Priest] and began to escort the two Sages. [Nearing their homes,] Shemayah and Avtalyon approached the High Priest to take their leave from him.

"May the sons of gentiles go in peace," he said condescendingly.

"The sons of gentiles who emulate Aaron[11] shall go in peace," they replied. "But the sons of Aaron who do not follow the ways of Aaron shall not go in peace" (*Talmud: Yoma* 71b).

---

10. Shemayah and Avtalyon, both descendants of converts, were the leading Torah Sages of Israel of that period.

11. The *kohanim* (priests) are paternal descendants of Moses's older brother Aaron. Through most of Israel's years of wandering in the desert, Aaron served as High Priest in the Tabernacle (*Mishkan*). He was known for his zealous pursuit of peace (note *Pirkei Avos* 1:12).

Maimonides' Letter to Obadiah the Righteous Convert

Thus says Moses, the son of Rabbi Maimon, one of the exiles from Jerusalem who lived in Spain:

I received the question of the master Obadiah, the learned and wise convert; may God reward him for what he has done, and may a perfect recompense be granted him by the Lord of Israel, under whose wings he has sought refuge.

You asked me if you, too, are allowed to say in the blessings and prayers you offer alone or with the congregation: "Our God, and God of our fathers," "You who have sanctified us through Your commandments," "You who have separated us," "You who have chosen us," "You who have taken us as an inheritance," "You who have brought us out of the land of Egypt," "You who have performed miracles for our fathers," and other such expressions.

You may say all this in the prescribed order and not change it in the least. Just as every Jew by birth says these blessings and prayers, so is it proper for you to bless and pray, whether you are alone or leading the congregation in prayer. The reason is that Abraham our Father taught all the people, enlightened them, and made known to them the true faith and the unity of God; he rejected the idols and abolished their worship; he brought many under the wings of the Divine Presence; he gave them counsel and advice and ordered his children and the members of his household after him to follow the path of God. As it is written in the Torah: "For I have known him to the end that he may command his children and his household after him, that they may keep the way of the Lord, to do righteousness and justice"

(Genesis 18:19). Therefore, throughout the generations, whoever embraces Judaism and professes the unity of the Divine name as prescribed by the Torah is counted among the disciples of Abraham our Father, peace be unto him. They are the members of Abraham's household, and it is as if he converted them to righteousness. Just as he converted his contemporaries through his words and teachings, so does he convert future generations through the testimony he left to his children and household after him. Thus, Abraham our Father, peace be unto him, is the father of his devout children who keep his ways, as well as the father of his disciples and all converts.

Therefore, you should pray, "Our God" and "God of our fathers," because Abraham, peace be unto him, is your father. You should pray, "You who have taken our fathers for His own possession," for the land was given to Abraham, as it states: "Arise, walk through the land in its length and in its breadth; for I shall give it to you" (Genesis 13:17). As for the words, "You who have brought us out of the land of Egypt," or "You who have performed miracles for our fathers," these you may change, if you like, and say, "You who have brought Israel out of the land of Egypt," and "You who have performed miracles for Israel." If, however, you do not change them, it is no transgression. Since you have come under the wings of the Divine Presence and professed your belief in God, no difference exists between you and us, and all miracles performed for us have been performed for you, as well.

Thus it states in the Book of Isaiah: "Neither let the son of the stranger that has joined himself to the Lord speak, saying, 'God has utterly separated me from His people'" (Isaiah 56:3). There is no difference whatever between you and us. You shall certainly say the blessing, "Who has chosen us," "Who has given us," "Who has separated us," "Who has taken us for Your own," "Who has separated us," for the Creator, may He be blessed, has indeed chosen you and separated you from the nations and given you the Torah. For the Torah has been given to us and to the converts, as it states: "One law shall there be, both for you of the congregation and also for the stranger who sojourns among you, an eternal ordinance throughout your generations; as you are, so shall the stranger be before God" (Numbers 15:15).

Know that our ancestors, when they came out of Egypt, were for the most part idolaters. They mingled with the pagans in Egypt and imitated their ways, until the Holy One, blessed be He, sent Moses our Teacher, the master of all prophets. He separated us from the nations and brought us under the wings of the Divine Presence, ourselves and all converts, and gave us all one Torah. Do not consider your origin as inferior. While we are descendants of Abraham, Isaac, and Jacob, you come from Him through whose utterance the world was created. As Isaiah states: "One shall say, I am the Lord's, and another shall call himself by the name of Jacob" (Isaiah 44:5) (Rabbi Moses Maimonides, *Teshuvos HaRambam* 293).

Seeking Proselytes

If one sees a place from which idol-worship has been up-rooted, he should say, "Blessed be He who has uprooted idol-worship from our land; and just as it has been uprooted from this place, so may it be uprooted from all places in the land of Israel; and may You turn the heart of those who serve them to serve You." Outside of the Holy Land it is not necessary to say, "May you turn the heart of those who serve them to serve You," because most of the people are idol-worshipers.

Rabbi Shimon Ben Elazar said: Even outside of the Holy Land one must recite these words, for [those who worship idols] are destined to convert, as it is written: "For then I shall convert the nations to a pure speech, that they shall all call upon the name of God" (*Talmud: Berachos* 57b, citing Zephaniah 3:9).

Commentary: Although ultimately our entire hope is for all the world to recognize and know the glory of God, there is no obligation whatever on our part to engage in proselytization. It is only incumbent upon us to disseminate the teachings of Torah and fear of Heaven among our own people. The perfection of the world under the Kingdom of the Almighty is one of the secrets of the Merciful One; only He knows the means by which He will enlighten the world at the time appointed for the end of darkness. Accordingly, [the first opinion cited above asserts that] we need not arouse our yearning for this ideal to the extent of establishing an obligatory prayer to be recited whenever we see a place from which idolatry has been uprooted. Although there are various allusions to this profound aspiration in the *"Aleinu"*

74

prayer, which is one of the highlights of the prayer service of both Rosh Hashanah (the Jewish New Year) and Yom Kippur (the Day of Atonement), these are but periodic reminders of our universal ideal. However, our standard blessings are not only concerned with such distant ideals, but also with practical ones. Hence, this [text] could lead one to err concerning our obligation to spread the knowledge of God among all the nations.

That is why, according to the first opinion, it is preferable not to establish [a reference to our ultimate ideal] as part of a standard blessing, for one might think that the obligation to focus upon it applies at all times. However, according to Rabbi Shimon Ben Elazar, even if we have no obligation or Divine imperative to proselytize other nations concerning faith and knowledge of God, clearly anything that hastens our redemption and elevates Israel and our Divine service will produce the further result that everyone in the world will perceive the glory of God's majesty by means of Israel.

This is axiomatic, because Israel is the unique channel for all the world to attain the knowledge of God. Accordingly, longing for the ultimate perfection of the world will arouse us speedily to complete [our own spiritual task] since [all the nations] are destined to convert. This conversion will be the consequence of their accepting the "yoke of the Kingdom of Heaven" through the intermediacy and influence of Israel. A strong proof for this is [the verse], "For then I shall convert the nations to a pure speech, that they shall all call upon the name of God to serve Him with a common accord" (Zephaniah 3:9).

This common accord (which is imperative) among those who serve God is of great universal human benefit, both spiritually and physically. [However,] it can only be derived from the source of Israel. This will be the one channel [of Divine truth] in the world; [from thence] it will divide into many paths according to the apprehension and nature of each and every nation and their innate ability to receive the light of the Torah of Israel. However, if it were possible for the nations to attain knowledge of God at the end of days, each according to its own intellectual apprehen-

sion and subsequently by their combination, all the nations
would still lack the "pure speech" by which to serve God with "a
common accord." For each nation is possessed of a different
spiritual essence; [therefore] their inclinations and viewpoints
differ. They require a great common denominator, especially
concerning perceptions of a spiritual nature.

Since the light of Israel will completely illuminate the entire
world, [Rabbi Shimon Ben Elazar asserts that] we are obliged to
include this matter in our standard prayers, that it may inspire
our deeds. As a result, through our intermediacy, the ultimate
purpose will be grasped in the most focused way. Thus, the
vineyard of the House of Israel itself will receive nurture [from
this reminder of its universal mission, even when it remains a
distant goal] (Rabbi Avraham Yitzchak Kook, *Ein Ayah, Berachos*
II:114).[12]

---

12. It could be argued that the Men of the Great Assembly established
numerous scriptural references to such universal ideals throughout the
communal prayer service. Thus, their concern with the possibility of Jews
having a beneficial spiritual influence on non-Jews is firmly rooted in tradition. In fact, since early medieval times it has been customary to conclude each
of the three daily prayer services with the "*Aleinu*" prayer, which, as Rabbi
Kook mentions, was originally recited on Rosh Hashanah and Yom Kippur
alone. However, in practice, most authorities share the more cautious position
regarding the Jewish mission to non-Jews voiced here by Rabbi Kook.

King Solomon's Prayer

[During the ceremonial dedication of the Holy Temple in Jerusalem, King Solomon included the following passage in his prayer:] Also the foreigner, who does not belong to Your people, Israel, who comes from a distant land for Your name's sake, because he heard of Your great name, Your mighty hand, and Your outstretched arm, and he comes and prays toward this house—may You take heed from Your heavenly dwelling place and fulfill all that the foreigner asks of You. Thus, all nations of the world may know Your name, in order to revere You, as does Your people Israel; and they will know that this house that I have built is called by Your name (I Kings 8:41–43).

Rabbi Yehoshua Ben Levi taught: If the nations of the world had known how beneficial the Holy Temple was for them, they would have surrounded it to protect it; for it was of greater benefit to them than to the Israelites. King Solomon prayed, "Also the foreigner who does not belong to Your people, Israel . . ." (I Kings 8:41). And it is written, "May You take heed from Your Heavenly dwelling place and fulfill all that the foreigner asks of You" (I Kings 8:43). But when it comes to the Israelites, what does it say? "[May You hear from Your dwelling place and forgive] and render unto everyone according to his ways, whose heart You know" (II Chronicles 6:30). If he is deserving, he shall receive; if not, he shall not receive (*Midrash: Numbers Rabba* 1:3).

The Holy Temple

And through you and your descendants shall all families of the earth be blessed (Genesis 28:14).

Commentary: As long as the Holy Temple stood, the seventy nations were blessed and sustained through the intercession of Israel, who offered seventy sacrifices on their behalf during the Festival of Booths (*Sukkah* 55b). Even during their exile, the Jewish people have greatly benefited the nations, as it is written, "They made me keeper of the vineyards" (Song of Songs 1:6) (Rabbi Chaim ibn Attar, *Ohr HaChaim*, ad loc.).

Jerusalem

Abba Isi Ben Yochanan cited Shmuel HaKatan as saying: The world is like the iris of a person's eye. The white part of the eye is the ocean that surrounds the land. The iris is the land. The pupil is Jerusalem. The image in the center of the pupil is the Holy Temple—may it be rebuilt speedily in our days and in the days of all Israel, amen (*Talmud: Derech Eretz Zuta* 9).

Just as the navel is located in the middle of the body, so is Israel located in the center of the world, as it is written, "The people who dwell in the navel of the earth" (Ezekiel 38:12). Jerusalem is in the center of Israel, the Holy Temple is in the middle of Jerusalem, and the Rock of the Temple Mount in front of the Ark is the place from which the world is nourished. [Since] the wise King Solomon understood that the roots of Jerusalem extend through the entire world, he planted all sorts of trees there and grew fruits. Thus, he declared, "I have made for myself gardens and orchards, and I planted in them every kind of fruit tree" (Ecclesiastes 2:5). (*Midrash Tanchuma, Kedoshim* 10).

Jerusalem is the light of the world, as it is written, "And nations will walk in your light" (Isaiah 60:3). And who is the light of

79

Jerusalem? The Holy One, blessed be He, as it is written, "And God will be for you an eternal light" (Isaiah 60:19). (*Midrash: Bereishis Rabba* 59:8).

"Arise, shine, for your light has arrived . . . And nations shall walk in your light, and kings in your shining brilliance" (Isaiah 60:1–3). Rabbi Hoshaya declared: Jerusalem is destined to become a lantern to the nations of the world, and they will walk in its light. How do we know this? [From the verse that states,] "And nations will walk in your light" (*Midrash: Yalkut Shimoni,* Isaiah 499).

In this world, the joy of all the world has ceased. And when the Holy One, blessed be He, will rebuild Jerusalem, He will restore the joy [of all the world] in its midst (*Midrash: Shemos Rabba* 52:5).

Rabban Shimon Ben Gamliel said: In the future all nations and governments will be gathered together in Jerusalem, as it states: "And all the nations shall be gathered unto her in the name of God" (Jeremiah 3:17). [This Talmudic Sage proves his interpretation by citing a similar scriptural usage.] Elsewhere it is written, "God declared: 'Let the waters be gathered together'" (Genesis 1:9). Just as the waters of creation were gathered into one place, so shall the assembly of nations and governments be gathered into Jerusalem, as the verse states, "And all the nations shall be gathered unto her" (*Baraisa: Avos D'Rabbi Nosson* 35:9).

"I am black but beautiful, O daughters of Jerusalem" (Song of Songs 1:5). Rabbi Yochanan [interprets "daughters of Jerusalem" as follows]: In the future Jerusalem will be a metropolis for all nations of the earth. This is comparable to the verse that states, "Ashdod and her daughters"[13] (*Midrash: Shemos Rabba* 23:10).

"Speak unto the heart of Jerusalem and call unto her that her mission has been fulfilled, that her sin has been pardoned; for she has won from the Lord's hand double for all her sins" (Isaiah 40:2).

Commentary: The prophet envisions the time when Israel, as the nation of *kohanim* (priests), will have accomplished its historic mission. Then Jerusalem will become the focal point, the heart of the world, to and from which life will stream, not only to Israel but to all mankind. This is the double portion, the immeasurably higher position that Jerusalem will occupy in comparison to that of the past. From [the city] that had been forsaken and misunderstood by her own children, all humanity will receive the pulse of life (Rabbi Mendel Hirsch, ad loc.).

The time is coming when I will gather all nations and tongues, and they shall come and see My glory. . . . And they shall bring your brothers from among the nations as an offering to God, upon horses and in chariots, in litters and upon mules and swift camels, to My holy mountain, Jerusalem, says God; just as the children of Israel bring an offering in a clean vessel to the house

---

13. The term "daughters" indicates the smaller settlements surrounding this city. Similarly, all the countries of the world will be called "daughters of Jerusalem" when world peace is established by the Messiah, who will rule from Jerusalem.

of God. And also from them shall I select priests and Levites, says God (Isaiah 66:18, 20, 21).

Commentary: I will appoint some of the gentiles who will bring the Jews back to the land of Israel as priests and Levites, as well as some of the Jews who until now had been forced to live in a state of ritual impurity in the diaspora. Before Me it is revealed who among them are priests and Levites; I will select them from their midst, and they shall serve before Me, says God. Concerning this, the verse states, "The hidden things belong to the Lord, our God" (Deuteronomy 29:28). Thus is this matter explained in the *Midrash Tehillim* (Rashi, ad loc.).

Enlightenment

[The Prophet Elijah declared]: I call heaven and earth to bear witness that anyone—Jew or gentile, man or woman, slave or handmaid—if his deeds are worthy, the Divine Spirit will rest upon him (*Midrash: Tanna D'vei Eliyahu Rabba* 9:1).

"And the glory of the Lord will be revealed, and all flesh will see it together" (Isaiah 40:5). The term "all flesh" comes to include non-Jews, as well. Thus the Jerusalem Talmud states: "Whether one hears the Divine name blasphemed by an Israelite or a non-Jew, one must rend his garments. Which verse proves this? 'I am God, the Lord of all flesh'" (Jeremiah 32:27, cited in *Yerushalmi Sanhedrin* 7:1). (Rabbi Yosef Rosen of Rogotchov, *Tzafnas Pane'ach, Devarim*, p. 26).

And afterward I shall pour forth My spirit upon all flesh, and all your sons and daughters will prophesy; your elders will dream dreams, your youths will see visions (Joel 3:1).

Commentary: "I shall pour forth My spirit." This refers to the spirit of wisdom and apprehension of Godliness. "Upon all flesh." For then the non-Jewish nations, too, will discern and know God (*Metzudas David*, ad loc.).

83

Although eternal life may be attained even in the present state of reality, it will primarily characterize the future, when spiritual knowledge will increase. At that time, everyone will know God—and, through this knowledge, everyone will be incorporated into the Divine Oneness. Then all creatures will live forever, like God. For by knowing God, everyone will be incorporated into Him, as the wise man remarked, "If I knew Him, I would be Him."[14] This spiritual knowledge will be in the future, as indicated by the verse, "The earth will be full of the knowledge of God" (Isaiah 11:9). Because of this knowledge, nothing will be lacking. Thus, the Midrash states, "If you possess knowledge, what do you lack? And if you lack knowledge, what do you possess?" (*Vayikra Rabba* 1:6). Everything will be completely good.

Even non-Jews will know God through this increase in spiritual knowledge—each person according to his own level and to whatever extent he exerted himself to serve God in this world. This is implied by the prophet's metaphor that the future knowledge of God will be like "the water that fills the sea." The sea is one; yet, due to the ocean's floor, it is deeper in one place than another. Thus, it shall be in the future: the depth of each person's knowledge of God will vary according to the nature and extent of his previous efforts in Divine service.

All of humanity will then live forever, for the knowledge of God will be revealed, and everyone will be incorporated in the Divine Oneness. Thus, on the verse, "On that day God will be One and His name One" (*Zechariah* 14:9), our Sages ask, "Is He now not One? But presently the blessing we recite upon hearing bad news is: 'Blessed be the True Judge,' whereas upon hearing good news we say: 'Blessed is the Beneficent One, Who does good.' However, in the future world, the latter blessing will be said at all times" (*Pesachim* 50a). This is because in the future,

---

14. *Kuzari* 5:21. In its original context, this aphorism underscores God's unknowability. Here, Chasidic master Rabbi Nachman of Breslov uses it to make the converse point.

when knowledge is revealed, it will be known that evil does not really exist; rather, everything is good, and everything is one.

Even the experience of exile is only due to our lack of spiritual knowledge. As the verse states, "Therefore have I exiled My people, who have no knowledge" (Isaiah 5:13). This is also why the redemption from Egyptian bondage came through Moses. [Since Moses was the greatest of the Prophets,] he personified the aspect of knowledge. Thus, it is written, "You will know that I am God, Who brings you out from under the subjugation of Egypt" (Exodus 6:7). For the main redemption is attained through knowledge (Rabbi Nachman of Breslov, *Likkutei Moharan* I:21, sect. 11–13, abridged).

Abraham's Other Son

Concerning the verse, "And Abraham said to his lads, 'Remain here with the donkey'" (Genesis 22:5), our Sages state: "This refers to people comparable to a donkey" (*Kiddushin* 65a). However, by this expression they did not mean that [Abraham's companions] were lacking in wisdom. Does not Scripture itself testify that Eliezer was among them, who was called "Eliezer the Damascan" (Genesis 15:2)? Our Sages interpret this to mean, "He drew (*doleh*) the waters of his master's teachings and enabled others to drink (*mashkeh*)."[15] [Thus, there is a seeming contradiction.] However, our Sages go on to explain themselves: since [Abraham's companions] did not see the cloud of the Divine Presence atop the mountain, they were called "people comparable to a donkey." "Just as a donkey does not see [sublime things], so do you [not see]" (*Kiddushin*, loc. cit.).

It might be objected that one's servants are sometimes termed acquisitions, like beasts and donkeys. Even according to this view, this euphemism might only be applied to Abraham's servant, Eliezer.[16] [However,] Ishmael his son was also there,

---

15. That is, the rabbis of the Talmud homiletically relate the Hebrew word *Dameshek* ("Damascan") to the words *doleh* ("drew") and *mashkeh* ("drink"). See *Yoma* 25b.

16. Note *Sefer HaGilgulim* of the Ari *z"l* (chap. 48), that due to his great spiritual merit, Abraham's servant Eliezer was reincarnated successively as Caleb Ben Yefuneh, Benayahu Ben Yohayada, and the Prophet Zechariah. The Ari *z"l* also states (chap. 65) that the master Kabbalist Rabbi Moshe Cordovero shared a common "soul-root" with Eliezer: specifically, he embodied the *ru'ach*

"Ishmael Ben Abraham," and a son is associated with the family of his father (Rabbi Chaim Vital, Introduction to *Sefer Eitz Chaim*, vol. I, Ashlag ed., p. 12a).

And these are the generations of Ishmael . . . (Genesis 25:12).

Commentary: This shows you the preciousness of Ishmael, in that the Torah enumerates the years of his life. Moreover, the phrase "and he was gathered unto his people" shows that he attained a lofty level in the World to Come[17] (Rabbi Avraham Maimonides, *Commentary on Genesis*, Bodelian ms. Hunt. 166).

(spirit) of Eliezer, which formerly had been present in the Prophet Zechariah. Also, a "spark" of Eliezer's soul was present in the Prophet Habbakuk and the Talmudic saint, Choni HaMagel, according to *Likkutei HaShas* of the Ari z"l, *Ta'anis*. The main point here is that, although there is a spiritual hierarchy in creation, it is possible to ascend from level to level.

17. Ishmael is traditionally identified as the progenitor of the Arab nations. Although Ishmael committed grave transgressions in his youth, he sincerely repented in his later years. See *Baba Basra* 16b; *Rashi* on Genesis 25:9; also note *Zohar* I:124b, I:205b, II:87a; Malbim on Zechariah 8:23 (end).

Non-Jews in the Holy Land

Our brothers, people of a certain place, come in peace (*Mishna: Bikkurim* 3:3).

Commentary: "Our brothers," you are united with us by the power of fraternity that is perfected in the centrality of the city of God, the holy mountain. Simultaneously, we recognize that you are also "people of a certain place," and we have no desire to divest you of your allegiance to the city in which you dwell, which must naturally be dear to you.

This approach acts also as an exercise and manual for the great universal peace that Israel should feel toward all the peoples according to God's Torah, "whose ways are ways of pleasantness and peace." "A stranger and resident, he will live among you" (Leviticus 25:35), says the Torah in relation to gentiles who live among us in our land. We insist only that he desist from an evil and injurious path and be a straight man according to the Noahide code. Inasmuch as he has a nation and homeland for which he longs and has affection, he is a "stranger"; nevertheless, the Torah recognizes him as a "resident" in terms of affability, freedom, and human rights. Let your heart not persuade you to rob him of his natural feelings for his people and land, making him simply a "resident." Rather, "a stranger and a resident, he will live among you."

In tandem with the general instruction regarding the nations of the world should be the specific instruction regarding the relation of the metropolis and its satellites. They should be as brothers united and at the same time mindful of the value of the place [of origin] and all its demands. This is the true, correct peace: "Our brothers, people of a certain place, come in peace" (Rabbi Avraham Yitzchak Kook, *Ein Ayah* on *Bikkurim* 3:3, as presented in Rabbi Bezalel Naor's *Of Societies Perfect and Imperfect*, pp. 32–34).

Other Religions

As for other religions, in my opinion, it is not the goal of Israel's light to uproot or destroy them, just as we do not aim for the general destruction of the world and all its nations, but rather their correction and elevation, the removal of their dross. Then, of themselves, they shall join the Source of Israel, from whence a dew of light will flow over them. "And I will take away the blood from his mouth and his detestable things from between his teeth, and he, too, shall remain for our God" (Zechariah 9:7). This applies even to idolatry—all the more so to those religions that are partially based upon the light of Israel's Torah.

Great are the words of the Vilna Gaon, of blessed memory: "And I hated Esau" (Malachi 1:3) refers to that which is inferior in Esau. However, that which is primary in him, his head, is [according to the Midrash] buried together with the Patriarchs of the world [in the Cave of Machpelah]. Hence, Jacob, the man of simplicity, the man of truth, said, "I beheld your face as if I beheld the face of God" (Genesis 33:10). And his words will not be left unfulfilled. The brotherly love of Esau [progenitor of the Christian nations] and Jacob, Isaac and Ishmael [progenitor of the Islamic nations] will rise above all those upheavals, above the evil consequences of the body's profane desires, and will overcome them and turn them into light and eternal loving kindness. This broad knowledge, sweetened in the honey of the Torah of Truth, must accompany us in all our paths at the End of Days, to seal the Torah in the Palace of the King, the Messiah, by turning "bitterness to sweetness and darkness to light" (*Zohar*, Introduction, 4a) (Rabbi Avraham Yitzchak Kook, *Igros LaRayah* 112).

ॐ

All these things concerning Jesus the Nazarene and Mohammed the Ishmaelite who arose after him only serve to pave the
way for the Messianic King, who will perfect the entire world and
bring all men to serve God in unison. It has thus been predicted:
"For then I will convert the nations to a pure language, that they
may all call upon the name of God and serve Him with a
common accord" (Zephaniah 3:4).

All nations will return to true faith and will no longer steal and
oppress. Together with Israel they will eat that which they have
honestly gained. This is what [Isaiah] means when he says, "The
lion shall eat straw like the ox" (Isaiah 11:7). All prophecies such
as these regarding the Messiah are allegorical. Only in the
Messianic era will we know the meaning of each allegory and
what it comes to tell us. . . .

Our Sages and Prophets did not long for the Messianic era in
order that they might rule the world and dominate the gentiles.
They did not desire that the nations should honor them, or that
they should eat, drink, and be merry. They only desired one
thing: to be free to involve themselves in the Torah and its
wisdom. They wanted nothing to disturb or distract them, in
order that they should become worthy of life in the World to
Come. . . .

In the Messianic era there will be neither war nor famine.
Jealousy and competition will cease to exist, for all good things
will be plentiful and all sorts of delicacies will be common as
dust. Humanity's main occupation will be only to know God. The
Jews will therefore become great Sages, knowing many hidden
things and attaining the greatest understanding of God possible
for a human being. The Prophet [Isaiah] thus predicted, "The
earth shall be full of the knowledge of God as the water covers the
sea" (Isaiah 11:9). (Maimonides, *Mishneh Torah*, Laws of Kings
11:4, 12:1–5, with *hashmatos*).

ॐ

Christians and Moslems must be regarded as an instrument for the fulfillment of the prophecy that the knowledge of God will one day spread throughout the earth. Whereas the nations before them worshiped idols, denied God's existence, and did not recognize God's power or His retribution, the rise of Christianity and Islam served to spread among the nations, to the farthest ends of the earth, the knowledge that there is One God Who governs the world, Who rewards and punishes and reveals Himself to man. Christian scholars have not only won acceptance among the nations for the revelation of the Written Law (the Torah) but have also helped to safeguard God's Oral Law (the Talmud and rabbinic tradition). For when, in their hostility to the Torah, ruthless persons in their own midst sought to abrogate and uproot the Talmud, others from among them arose to defend it and to repulse these attempts (Rabbi Yaacov Emden on *Pirkei Avos* 4:13).

Tikkun Olam: Perfecting the World

Nations shall walk in your light, and kings in your shining brilliance (Isaiah 60:3).

Commentary: They will learn God's ways from you, and you will enlighten them (*Metzudas David*, ad loc.).

If a Jew sees a non-Jew committing a transgression and it is possible to deter him, he should do so. Thus did the Holy One, blessed be He, send the Prophet Jonah to Nineveh to return [the non-Jewish inhabitants of that city] to the proper path. When God is displeased with one nation, it is difficult for others to entreat Him, as well (Rabbi Yehudah HeChasid, *Sefer Chasidim* 1124).

I heard in the name of Rabbi Yisrael Baal Shem Tov [founder of the Chasidic movement] that when the Seven Universal Laws were given to the descendants of Noah, the [souls of the] Jewish people agreed to become guarantors for the rest of the world (*Rav Yaivi, Vayeishev*).

[Our Sages taught that] every person must say, "The whole world was created for my sake" (*Sanhedrin* 37a). Therefore, since

93

the whole world was created for my sake, I must always be concerned with improving the world, fulfilling the needs of humanity, and praying for its benefit (Rabbi Nachman of Breslov, *Likkutei Moharan* I, 5:1).

The greatness of the Holy One, blessed be He, is primarily [revealed] when the gentile nations, too, come to know that there is a Divine Master and Ruler. As the *Zohar* states: When Jethro came and said, "Now I know that God is great" (Exodus 18:11), the supernal name became endeared and exalted (*Zohar* II, *Yisro*, 69a). (Rabbi Nachman of Breslov, *Likkutei Moharan* I, 10:1).

In the Ultimate Future, speech will be perfected. Even the non-Jewish nations will use their power of speech to call out to God, as it is written, "For then I will convert the nations to a pure speech, that they shall all call upon the name of God" (Zephaniah 3:9). Thus, speech will be perfected. At present, speech is lacking and incomplete, for the whole world is not using the power of speech to call out to God. However, in the Ultimate Future, they will all use the power of speech to call out to God, even the non-Jewish nations. Then speech will be perfected. This is the aspect of "a pure speech," since everyone will use speech to call out to God (Rabbi Nachman of Breslov, *Likkutei Moharan* I, 66:3).

One must not let the world fool him, for no one ends up well in this world. All people, even those who possess everything the world has to offer, eventually experience great suffering. The suffering of one generation affects the next generation as well.

The nations of the world also need to realize this.[18] Since the world's allurements are really of no worth, what should they do with their lives? For this, they must have great merit—to know their true calling in life. However, Israel has been spared this dilemma, for they already know what to do through the Torah (Rabbi Nachman of Breslov, *Sichos HaRan* 51).

When the Jewish people do not make Godliness known to the nations of the world, [this creates a spiritual vaccum]. As a result, the nations induce them to follow ideologies contrary to the Torah (Rabbi Nachman of Breslov, *Sefer HaMidos, Emunah* II:11).

The completion of faith and its "jewelled ornaments" are obtained when the very people who were most distant [from holiness] are drawn close. Thus, it is written, "[For then I will convert the nations to a pure language,] that they may all call upon the name of God . . ." (Zephaniah 3:9). Even the idolatrous nations will draw close to the faith of Israel, "and they will serve Him with a common accord" (Rabbi Nachman of Breslov, *Likkutei Moharan* I, 62:3).

It is necessary to reveal to all of humanity, from the greatest to the humblest individual, that there is a Creator. Therefore, the Torah was given in written form. By writing, which is a physical act, the light of this perception—faith in God—is drawn into the physical world. Thus the ultimate purpose of creation is fulfilled:

---

18. In *Likkutei Halachos* (*Even HaEzer*), *P'ru U'Rivu* 3:34, a slightly different version of this teaching is given. There it seems to suggest that it is Israel's spiritual task to make this known to the rest of the world.

that all people should apprehend God's Oneness (Rabbi Nosson Sternhartz, *Likkutei Halachos, Kiddushin* 3:1).

Every Jew must encourage others to return to God and to engage in Divine service, for this is the true basis of civilization (Rabbi Nosson Sternhartz, *Likkutei Eitzos HaMeshulosh, Geirim* 17).

The future redemption will apply not only to Israel, but to the whole world as well. As we say in the *Aleinu* prayer, ". . . to perfect the world under the sovereignty of God." In preparation for this redemption, therefore, action needs to be taken so that the world at large will be ready for such a state. This is to be achieved through the efforts of the Jewish people to influence the nations of the world to conduct themselves in the spirit of the verse which states that God "formed [the world] in order that it be settled" (Isaiah 45:18)—in a civilized manner, through the observance of their seven commandments (Rabbi Menachem M. Schneerson of Lubavitch, *Likkutei Sichos, Beshalach* 5743 [1983]).

The mission and purpose of the Jew is to make this world a dwelling place for God. The world, which seems to run according to its own natural laws, is not independent. It has a Creator, who has not left it unattended. God is on earth as He is in heaven.

The Jew, through his Divine service, demonstrates that the spiritual and the physical can be brought together. The mundane can be sanctified, and everyday life can become holy. God dwells in the world.

An integral component of the Jew's task is to bring it about that all people, not only Jews, acknowledge God as Creator and Ruler of the world. The world, we are told, "was not created for chaos, but that it be inhabited." A chaotic world results when there are no absolute criteria by which to live, when morals and ethics are based solely on man's understanding. Man is swayed by interests other than reason and justice; we have too recently seen the destruction that ensues when laws and philosophy are perverted to serve personal ends.

God, the Creator of the world, has not abandoned His handiwork, but has given clear guidance as to how the world can be made "inhabited," settled and productive, decent and enduring. The nations of the world have been given a Divine code of conduct—the Seven Laws of Noah. This code consists of six prohibitions, against murder, robbery, idolatry, adultery, blasphemy, cruelty to animals, and one positive commandment, to establish a judicial system. These Seven Laws of Noah are general precepts, which, with their ramifications and extensions, encompass countless details.

The reason these seven laws are to be observed is also important. Maimonides rules that the Children of Noah [i.e., all humanity] must observe these laws because "God commanded them in the Torah and informed us through Moses that the Children of Noah had already been so commanded" (*Mishneh Torah*, Laws of Kings 8:11). A non-Jew conducts himself in consonance with the Seven Laws of Noah not because human logic compels him to do so, but because they are God's commandments transmitted through Moses. This ensures that self-interest will never be allowed to pervert the Divine criteria of human conduct.

It is through the observance of the Seven Laws of Noah that the entire world becomes a decent, productive place, a fitting receptacle for the Divine. Then, Scripture promises, "the glory of the Lord will be revealed, and all flesh together will see that the mouth of the Lord has spoken." The culmination of this will be the Messianic era, when, through the agency of the Messiah, "all will call in the name of the Lord and serve Him with a common accord" (Rabbi Menachem M. Schneerson of Lubavitch, *Likkutei Sichos*, 11 Nissan 5743 [1983]).

Exile and Redemption

Rabbi Chizkiah taught: The Holy One, blessed be He, sent the Jewish people into exile only so that through them the nations of the world would receive blessing (*Zohar* I, *Vayechi* 244a).

God has a secret and wise design concerning the Jewish people. This may be compared to the wisdom hidden in a seed that falls to the ground, where it undergoes an external transformation through its contact with earth, water, and dung, until it is virtually unrecognizable. However, it is the seed itself that transforms earth and water to its own substance, carrying them from one level to another until it refines these elements and transmutes them to its own form. [The emerging plant] must cast off its husk, leaves, etc., until the heart has been purified and refined and is fit to bear the Divine influence. Thus does the original seed produce a tree that bears fruit like itself. Similarly, all religions that came after the Torah of Moses are part of the process of bringing humanity closer to the essence of Judaism— even though they may appear to be antithetical to it.

[This analogy also describes the relationship between the nations and Israel throughout history, culminating in the Messianic era.] The nations serve to introduce and pave the way for the long-awaited Messiah. He is the fruit, and they, in turn, will all [be transformed and] become his fruit when they acknowledge him. Then all nations will become one tree, recognizing the common root that they had previously scorned (Rabbi Yehudah HaLevi, *Kuzari* IV:23).

"The Holy One, blessed be He, acted charitably toward His people by dispersing them among the nations of the world" (*Pesachim* 87b). This dispersal enables the Jewish people to elevate and refine all the seventy nations[19] by means of the Torah they study and the commandments they fulfill wherever they are scattered. And this is why, when the Messiah appears, all the nations of the world will gather around him, as it is written, "He will have a gathering of nations" (*Bereishis* 49:10). (Rabbi Dov Ber of Lubavitch, *Toras Chaim, Shemos* 335b).

---

19. According to rabbinic tradition, there are seventy primary nations aside from the nation of Israel.

Return to God

"If you will return, O Israel," declares the Lord, "return to Me; and if you remove your abominations from before Me, without vacillating, and if you will swear, 'As God lives,' in truth, in justice, and in righteousness, the nations shall bless themselves in Him, and in Him they shall glory" (Jeremiah 4:1–2).

Commentary: When Israel will sincerely return to God and follow the Torah's precepts, joy and well-being will spread far beyond the Jewish sphere and fill the whole world (Rabbi Mendel Hirsch, ad loc.).

The Festival of Tabernacles (Succos) is called "the season of our rejoicing"; it is a foretaste of the bliss of the World to Come. In this world, joy is not complete. Thus, it is written, "God will rejoice in His works" (Psalms 104:31), concerning which our Sages explain, "The verse does not say 'rejoices' in the present tense but 'will rejoice,' anticipating the future" (*Midrash Tanchuma, Acharei* 2). It is also written, "Light is sown for the righteous" (Psalms 97:11). This world is dark and lacks light— only through the Divine commandments is "light sown for the righteous." However, [the verse continues,] "And joy for those whose hearts are straight." When the world has been restored to its original state of perfection—as the verse states, "The Lord made man straight (*yashar*)" (Ecclesiastes 7:29)—then joy, too, will be complete.

The Jewish people are granted a foretaste of this future state through the power of returning to God (*teshuvah*). [Three propitious times for this act of return are the three biblically mandated festivals of Passover, Shavuos, and Succos.] These festivals correspond to three names of the Jewish people: Jacob, Israel, and Jeshurun. "Jacob" is associated with that Patriarch's struggle with his rival brother, Esau. Therefore, Passover, the Festival of Freedom, alludes to the name of Jacob, in that it commemorates our exodus from captivity and servitude. Shavuos, the Festival of Weeks, commemorates the Giving of the Torah. It corresponds to the name "Israel," which contains the same Hebrew letters as the phrase, "*Li rosh*—a head unto Me." This [dedication to God] enables the Jewish people to cling fast to the Tree of Life (i.e., the Torah). The name "Jeshurun" corresponds to Succos, the Festival of Joy. [As the verse cited above suggests, this name] refers to the World to Come. When the Jewish people sincerely return to God, the crookedness of the human heart will be made straight (*yashar*). [Then joy will be complete, for it will be shared by all mankind] (Rabbi Yehudah Aryeh Leib Alter of Ger, *S'fas Emes, Inyan Succos*, p. 115b).

Divine Service

"Whatever the Holy One, blessed be He, created in His world, He created for His glory, as it is said: 'Everything that is called by My name was created for My glory; I have formed it; yea, I have made it' (Isaiah 43:7). And it is said: 'The Lord shall reign forever and ever' (Exodus 15:18). (*Mishna: Avos* 6:11).

Commentary: This tractate of the Mishna, which is devoted to the wisdom of our Sages, concludes with the thought that the purpose of all creatures, not only the Jewish people, is to serve God (Rabbi Samson Raphael Hirsch, ad loc.).

Disseminating the Seven Laws of Noah

The Jewish people are often divided into two categories [symbolized by the ancient tribes of] Issachar and Zebulun. [The members of Issachar were Torah scholars, whereas those of Zebulun were merchants. Because the merchants helped support the Torah scholars, they also possessed a share in the latter's spiritual merits.]

There was a time when Torah scholars had no secular involvements. For example, Rabbi Shimon Bar Yochai and his colleagues did not desist from Torah study for even a moment. "Torah was their only occupation," [the Talmud informs us]. In contrast, today, even the most learned and holy members of the Jewish people are somewhat involved in business or at least come in contact with secular society. They must realize that their involvement with non-Jews is not coincidental but has a Divine purpose: that they may influence those non-Jews to observe the Seven Laws of Noah.

If this applies to the "Issachars," the Torah scholars of our day, it surely has relevance to the "Zebuluns," the businessmen, who in many cases conduct most of their affairs together with non-Jews. They should not only receive from their non-Jewish acquaintances, but also give, by teaching them Torah values.

Furthermore, there are many whom God has granted positions of influence and power in secular society, as well as connections with city and local governments. It is their responsibility to use that influence and those connections for the sake of Judaism and for the benefit of the world at large by endeavoring to spread harmony in the world, [which is the aim of the Seven Laws of Noah]. By not doing so, one renounces the potential God has granted him. This is clearly in violation of the ruling of Maimonides [that every Jew must try to influence non-Jews to recognize the Creator and observe the Seven Laws of Noah].

The fact that such an individual does not utilize the potential granted him [to further this universal mission] has a negative effect upon the Jewish people as well. At the very beginning of our exile, we were told by the Prophet Jeremiah, "Seek the peace of the city . . . for in its peace, you shall have peace." Thus, it is clear that when the peace of the cities in which we dwell will be secured through the observance of the Seven Laws of Noah, the peace of the Jewish people will also increase (Rabbi Menachem M. Schneerson of Lubavitch, *Likkutei Sichos*, 19 *Kislev* 5743 [1982]).

Chasidic Teachings for Non-Jews

The "spreading of the wellsprings" of Chasidic teachings should not be limited to Jews alone, but should be extended outward to non-Jews as well. As [Maimonides] states, the purpose of giving the Torah was to bring peace to the world (*Mishneh Torah*, Laws of Chanukah 4:14). Similarly, he writes that every Jew is obligated to try and influence those who are not Jewish to fulfill the Seven Laws of Noah. Maimonides also states that one of the achievements of the Messiah will be to spiritually refine and elevate the nations of the world until they, too, become aware of God, to the point where Godliness will be revealed "to all flesh," [a term which denotes both Jews and] non-Jews.

Since the rewards of Torah come "measure for measure," it follows that among the efforts to bring the Messianic age must be the effort to spread the Seven Laws of Noah, as well as the wellsprings of Chasidic teachings associated with them, outward to non-Jews. Indeed, the Prophets tell us, "Nations shall walk in your light." Although the Torah was given to the people of Israel, it will also serve as a light to the nations (Rabbi Menachem M. Schneerson of Lubavitch, *Likkutei Sichos*, 19 *Kislev* 5743 [1982]).

A Universal Message

When [Chasidic master Rabbi Nachman of Breslov] was sitting in his carriage on his way to Novaritch, he remarked: "I have the ability to change the whole world for the better. Not only common folk, but I could even change the righteous and other great people; for even the righteous need to improve themselves. Not only Israel, the holy nation, but I could bring all the nations of the world back to God. I could lead them on a path close to the religion of Israel. However, 'it is enough for a servant to be like his master'"[20] (*Berachos* 58b) (*Chayei Moharan* 251).

---

20. That is, the time had not yet arrived to undertake this task.

Post-Holocaust Universalism

On the one hand, Judaism speaks of the Torah as a private covenant with the Jewish people: "He has revealed His word to Jacob, His laws and decrees to Israel. He has done this for no other nation" (Psalms 147:19–20). On the other, it projects the values of Torah against the backdrop of mankind. "Observe them carefully," says Moses about the commandments, "for this is your wisdom and understanding in the eyes of the nations. They will surely hear all these rules and say: 'This great nation is surely a wise and understanding people'" (Deuteronomy 4:6). A Jewish perspective is both inward and outward, concerned to maintain a critical distance from other cultures, while at the same time engaging their attention and ultimate admiration. To be a Jew is to be a witness to the world of the presence of God.

It is a difficult challenge, and there are two quite different ways of abdicating from it. One is assimilation: the way of total integration. The other is withdrawal from society: the way of total segregation. These are opposite but not equal alternatives. Assimilation leads to Jewish extinction. Withdrawal may be a mode of Jewish survival. But the fact that segregation is infinitely preferable to assimilation does not thereby entail that it is ideal. It is not. For Jews are summoned to something altogether more vast than mere survival. They are called upon to play a specific part in the development of human civilization as a whole. That universal vision was never wholly absent from the Jewish imagination, though there were some ages in which it was less relevant than others.

It is extraordinarily relevant today. Western societies generally have moved from monolithic to pluralist cultures. The Jewish voice on ethical issues is sought and given an attentive hearing. The state of Israel is looked to as a model of democracy and civil liberties in the Middle East. That it is sometimes judged by friends and critics alike by a different standard from that applied to its neighbors is a phenomenon that should be seen for what it is: an implicit ethical compliment. Jews today are faced with possibilities for *kiddush Hashem* (sanctification of God's name) of which Hirsch, a century and a half ago, could only dream. That this ideal should be treated with skepticism, above all in Orthodox circles, is not only religiously tragic. It is in the long term unwise.

For if Judaism, either in Israel or in the diaspora, fails to win the admiration of observers, it will fail ultimately to win the emulation of Jews themselves. Jewish survival, that miraculous succession of defiances of probability, depends on more than the pursuit of survival as an end in itself. It depended, classically, on the pursuit of a vision of a holy people whose fidelity would one day lead the world to God. However difficult that vision is to sustain in a post-Holocaust world, it must be attempted, for it is essential to Jewish self-definition (Rabbi Jonathan Sacks, *Tradition in an Untraditional Age*, "An Agenda of Future Jewish Thought," pp. 111–112).

A Common Accord

The absolute belief in one God that is the basis of Israel's spiritual value system emphasizes the unity of life on earth through the power of the spirit. On the other hand, the civilizations arising from other nations are oriented to earthly conditions and constraints. Unfortunately, these lead to double standards of morality and life, which create a gulf in understanding. . . .

The only solution for establishing true harmony between Israel and the other nations is to raise all of mankind to Israel's ideal. This cannot be done by force, but will happen by itself through historical necessity. Whether realizing it or not, since the dawn of time humanity has been committed to this unification. Swept along by an irresistible force, it has cast off the different forms of paganism and idol-worshiping. It is progressively surmounting the religious systems that place intermediaries between the human soul and God. It is gradually triumphing over regimes that divide society into master and slave. Instinctively, it is moving toward the union of all men and all peoples in an era of justice and peace, an era crowned by the Kingdom of God.

Thus, the paths of Israel and the other nations are gradually coming together. The day will surely come when these paths will join. This must happen, because truth, which is the same for all nations, must triumph. The suspicion felt by the other nations toward Israel will be replaced by respect and recognition of Israel as the keeper of the flame of eternal truth over thousands of years. Then hearts will open wide, and Israel will share its spiritual heritage with all the nations and will offer them the universal framework for building the Kingdom of God.

In the final analysis, it is the reconciliation between Israel and the other nations that will bring about the restoration of universal harmony. For the achievement of Israel's ideal will result in the merging of all spheres of life—physical, ethical, spiritual, social, economic and political—into a grand and powerful unity. That cosmic harmony will embrace all men and all of nature. Out of the brotherhood of all creatures will spring up the common worship of one God, the Father of all mankind. And so the ancient prophecy of Zechariah (14:9) will be fulfilled, "The Lord will be King over all the earth; on that day the Lord will be One, and His name will be One" (Rabbi Elie Munk, *Ascent to Harmony* III:7).

2

The Chosen People

INTRODUCTION

For most humanists, Judaism's concept of a "chosen people" pushes all the wrong buttons. Assimilated secular Jews probably find the idea even more troubling than do their non-Jewish counterparts. Nevertheless, for nearly two thousand years, most of the Western civilized world has tacitly accepted that the Jews have a special relationship with God. Millions of Christians (and Torah-observant Jews) still do. In fact, it has been persuasively argued that this belief underlies many diverse expressions of anti-Semitism.[1] Given both the religious and historical consequences of this concept, it deserves to be properly understood.

Our selections reflect three basic premises: 1) that the doctrine of Israel as a "chosen people" does not deny that other individuals may establish a profound relationship with God; 2) that it neither dehumanizes the "unchosen," nor does it set them up to be

---

1. See Praeger and Telushkin's *Why the Jews?* (Simon and Schuster, 1983).

exploited; 3) that this doctrine has, in fact, its own deeply universalist implications.

If the Jewish people are mandated to become a spiritual elite, it is an elite that anyone can join. In the eyes of the Torah and Israel, a legitimate convert to Judaism is equal to any other Jew. "There shall be one law for the native-born and the proselyte" (Exodus 12:49). This principle is stated repeatedly throughout the Torah. Also, the Torah itself offers a "sister religion" to Judaism for those who do not wish to convert, but nevertheless seek an intimate relationship with God. In the Talmud, this is known as the path of the Children of Noah. The basis of the Noahide religion is the Universal Code, outlined in the second section of this book. Many non-Jews who believe in God but do not follow a particular organized religion have instinctively come close to this approach on their own. Our final point is that the role of Israel as the "chosen people" is not self-serving but ultimately leads to the benefit of all mankind.

In order to further understand the role of Israel in history, it is necessary to become familiar with some of the Torah's teachings.[2] It is a basic principle of Judaism that God created the universe in order to confer His goodness upon His creatures. Thus, it is written, "God is good to all, and His mercy is upon all His works" (Psalms 145:9).[3] In order to do so, God endowed mankind with freedom of choice. By overcoming the negative aspects of human nature, our spiritual reward is comparable to "earned bread" rather than "bread of shame."[4] The greatest possible gift is to

---

2. For an outline of Judaism's eschatology from a Kabbalistic perspective, see Rabbi Moshe Chaim Luzzatto's *Derech Hashem* (*The Way of God*), part I, sect. 2.

3. Also note *Emunos V'Deos* 1:4; *Zohar* I:10b; *Derech Hashem* 1:2; *Tanya, Shaar HaYichud V'ha'Emunah* 4. With a slightly different nuance, *Likkutei Moharan* I:64 states that God's original purpose was to bestow His mercy.

4. Rabbi Moshe Chaim Luzzatto, *Daas Tevunos* (*The Knowing Heart*); also see Tosefos on *Kiddushin* 36b, citing *Yerushalmi Orlah* 1:3; *Midbar Kadmos* of

enable a receiver to become a giver, too. This is God's gift to every human being, and it is the underlying purpose of all the challenges we face. By choosing the good of our own volition, we become "partners with God in creation."[5]

The Torah recounts the various transgressions of the first ten generations, due to which humanity was almost completely destroyed by the famous biblical flood. Through Noah and his family, the world was renewed. In a sense, they were a "chosen people." (In fact, according to the master Kabbalist Rabbi Isaac Luria, the souls of the generation of the flood were not utterly destroyed but were reincarnated as the Jewish people, and Noah was reincarnated as Moses[6].) Following the example and teachings of Noah, his contemporaries and descendants had the potential to restore the original spiritual purity of man and nature. In the Jewish mystical tradition, this act of rectification is called *tikkun*.

Ten generations later, however, the moral condition of humanity had greatly degenerated. Therefore, God created a core group of people who would accomplish the *tikkun* that the rest of humanity had come to forget. Rabbi Moshe Chaim Luzzatto compares the development of humanity to the growth of a tree. The first generations are analogous to roots and later generations to branches. During the era of the "roots" (which lasted until the generation of the Tower of Babel), all humanity could have permanently regained the status of Adam before the sin. Thereafter, the era of the "branches" began. The world was divided into the various nations, each possessing its own qualities and talents. However, one nation was uniquely dedicated to God. Through

---

the Chida, citing a dialogue between Rav Yosef Karo and his angelic mentor in *Maggid Mesharim, Bereishis.*

5. This is the paradigm of the *tzaddik*, the true servant of God, who has completely overcome his lower nature. See *Shabbos* 10a, 119b; *Megilla* 18a; *Bereishis Rabba* 79:10, 98:1 and 4, ed. with *Ein Chanoch*; *Vayikra Rabba* 36:4; *Esther Rabba* 1; *Zohar* I, 5a. This is discussed from a Chasidic point of view in Rabbi Gedaliah Kenig's *Chayei Nefesh.*

6. *Shaar HaPesukim, Shemos,* p. 102.

their efforts they would accomplish not only their own perfection but elevate the rest of creation as well. At this point, Abraham, the first Patriarch, emerged. Through Abraham and his wife, Sarah, the people of Israel began to be built up.[7]

Righteous individuals of former times, such as Noah, had inherited a tradition of belief in God, despite the decadence that surrounded them. Abraham, by contrast, was born into an environment of idolatry and had to search for God on his own.[8] For this reason, he and his wife, Sarah, are considered the parents of all converts to Judaism.[9] Their spiritual struggles and successes, as well as those of the other Patriarchs and Matriarchs, are imprinted in the bodies and souls of their descendants. Thus, the people of Israel are uniquely empowered for the great challenges of their role in history.

The rabbis also pointed out another important difference between Abraham and Noah. Whereas Noah was an outstanding example of righteousness in his generation, he did not go out of his way to edify or correct anyone else. Abraham cared about all of humanity—his righteousness possessed universalism.[10] And, what is more, he was prepared to risk his honor, his life, and even the life of his and Sarah's only son, Isaac, in fulfilling the Divine will. This selflessness is an essential prerequisite for the realization of God's Oneness and the consequent ability to relate to all beings with true compassion.

When Moses and the Children of Israel received the Torah at Mount Sinai, the Jewish people came into actual existence. Essentially, their task was not to become a nation like any other, but to attain holiness. What the Patriarchs and Matriarchs had

---

7. *Derech Hashem* 2:4.

8. Thus, the verse states in Ezekiel 33:24, "Abraham was one," i.e., he stood alone with God. See *Likkutei Moharan* II, *Hashmata* before Torah 1.

9. *Sukkah* 49b; *Bereishis Rabba* 39, 84; also note *Kiddushas Levi, Lech Lecha.*

10. *Zohar* I, *Noach* 58b; *Kiddushas Levi, Noach* (beginning); also note *Ha'amek Davar, Pesichah* to *Bereishis*; however, for a contrary view, see *Sanhedrin* 108a.

accomplished as individuals, they would accomplish as a nation. Moreover, as a paradigm for all humanity, Israel was empowered to bring creation back to its state of *tikkun*.

The Sages draw an analogy between Mount Sinai and the Holy Temple in Jerusalem.[11] Just as Moses ascended the heights of the mountain to intercede for the people, so did the *Kohen Gadol* (High Priest) enter into the Holy of Holies on the Day of Atonement in the Temple. Just as the Ten Commandments resounded from the heavens above Sinai, so did prophecy issue forth from between the two angelic forms over the Ark of the Covenant.[12] (The Ark of the Covenant was so called because it contained the tablets upon which the Ten Commandments were inscribed and the original Torah scroll written by Moses.[13]) As a vehicle of atonement, the Temple effected spiritual purification for all who sought to draw closer to God. As the locus of prophetic revelation, the Temple was intended to be a catalyst for the world's long-sought *tikkun*. Thus, the Midrash symbolically identifies the Holy Temple as the beginning point of creation and equates it to the entire world.[14]

The key figure in establishing the Kingdom of Israel with Jerusalem as its capitol was King David, through whom the potential for rectifying the fallen state of man reached a high point. He and his son, King Solomon, built the Holy Temple and,

---

11. *Midrash Tehillim* 87:3; *Zohar* I, *Vayeitzei* 149a; Nachmanides, *Commentary on the Torah*, intro. to *Sefer Vayikra* and gloss on *Vayikra* 1:1; ibid., intro. to *Sefer Bamidbar*; *Likkutei Halachos, Eiruvei Techumin* 4:9.

12. Exodus 25:22; *Bereishis Rabba* 70:8 regarding the Holy Temple in general; *Derashos HaRan* 8, p. 128; also see Abarbanel on I Samuel 4:4 and II Samuel 6:2.

13. *Devarim Rabbah* 9:4, ed. with *Ein Chanoch*; *Midrash Tehillim* 90:3. The Babylonian Talmud states (*Baba Basra* 14a) that both sets of tablets were kept in the Ark and debates whether or not the original Torah scroll was kept there as well. The Jerusalem Talmud (*Shekalim* 6:1) and *Yalkut Shimoni* (2:101) both state that there were two separate Arks, one containing the fragments of the first set of tablets and the other containing the second tablets and the Torah scroll written by Moses.

14. *Tanchumah, Pekudei* 3.

however briefly, established a reign of peace. Four hundred years later, due to the increasing moral decline of the nation, the first Temple was destroyed, and the Israelites were exiled by the conquering Babylonians. Subsequently, the Prophet Ezra led a number of exiles back to the Holy Land and, together with the men of the Great Assembly, reestablished society on the foundations of Torah. The Temple was rebuilt, and for several hundred years Israel flourished. However, a spirit of causeless hatred arose among the people; various political and religious factions began to contend with one another, until, at last, the Roman legions conquered the land. The Jewish Commonwealth and, eventually, the second Holy Temple were destroyed. Thus, the hope of ultimate *tikkun* was not realized, and a new phase of history began: the great exile of the Jews throughout the world.

By struggling to serve God in the darkness of His self-concealment, the Jewish people would be purified of their dross, in order to become a vessel of lasting worth. There is a principle in Torah that an evil deed is truly expiated only when a person finds himself in a situation similar to the one in which he erred and this time does not make the same mistake.[15] Through their many acts of penitence and self-sacrifice in exile, the Jews have accomplished a tremendous *tikkun* for themselves and all humanity—although this will not be apparent until the Messianic era. Then "night will shine like day, and darkness will shine like light"; the process of *tikkun* will be complete.[16]

Like Abraham, the nation of Israel has not only dedicated itself to God but also possesses universality. By the example and influence of the Jewish people, others have been brought back to God. This process will culminate in the time of which the Prophet said: "The mountain of God's House shall be established above the peaks and raised up above the heights, and all the nations shall flow to it" (Isaiah 2:2). At last, the world will attain

---

15. *Sichos HaRan* 71; also note *Yoma* 86b; *Mishneh Torah, Hilchos Teshuvah* 2:1.

16. See *Zohar* II, *Bo* 38a, citing Psalms 139:12.

its *tikkun*, and all souls will grasp the purpose for which they were created: the perception of Godliness. Then the Divine promise to Abraham will be fulfilled: "And through your seed shall all the nations of the world be blessed" (Genesis 22:18).

SOURCES

Not Because You Were Greater

Not because you were greater than all the nations did God desire you and choose you—for you are the least (*me'at*) of all the nations (Deuteronomy 7:7).

Talmud: Rabbi Yochanan taught in the name of Rabbi Elazar, son of Rabbi Shimon [Bar Yochai]: The Holy One, blessed be He, said to Israel, "I desire you because even when I bestow greatness upon you, you make yourselves small (*me'at*) before Me. I bestowed greatness upon Abraham, yet he said to Me, 'I am but dust and ashes' (Genesis 18:27); upon Moses and Aaron, yet they said, 'And we are nothing' (Exodus 16:8); and upon David, yet he said, 'But I am a worm and not a man'" (Psalms 22:7). (*Talmud: Chullin* 89a).

Midrash: Not because you are greater than the other nations, and not because you fulfill more commandments than them [have you been chosen]. For the other nations gratuitously perform more commandments than you, and they publicize My name more than you, as the verse states, "From the rising of the sun until it goes down, My name is great among the nations" (Malachi 1:11). "For you are the least (*me'at*)." However, because you make yourselves small (*me'at*) before Me, I love you (*Midrash Tanchuma, Ekev* 3).

The Divine Witness

And if a soul transgresses and hears the voice of warning—if one is a witness, whether he sees or otherwise knows, if he does not testify, he shall bear his iniquity (Leviticus 5:1).

Midrash: "You are My witness," the Lord declares, "and I am God" (Isaiah 43:10). If you do not proclaim Me as God to the nations of the world, you shall bear your iniquity (*Vayikra Rabba* 6:5).

Universal Benefit

God gave the Torah to the Jewish people so that all nations might benefit by it (*Midrash Tanchuma, Devarim* 3).

Just as [the sacrifice of] a dove atones for transgression, so does Israel atone for the nations of the world (*Midrash: Shir HaShirim Rabba* I:63, ed. with *Ein Chanoch*).

The Heart of the World

Israel among the nations is like the heart among the organs of the body. It is the healthiest, as well as the one most prone to disease. The verse states, "Only you have I known from all the families of the earth; therefore shall I punish you for your iniquities" (Amos 3:2). These [iniquities] are the sicknesses. However, concerning its health, our Sages declared: "He forgives the sins of His people, removing them one by one" (*Selichos*). God does not allow our sins to become overwhelming, lest they destroy us completely (Rabbi Yehudah HaLevi, *Kuzari* II:36).

Dedication to God

You have been chosen by the Lord, your God, to be His treasured people (Deuteronomy 7:6).

Commentary: For you have no chief, overseer, or ruler (Proverbs 6:7) among all the angels on high, but you are the treasure (*segula*) of God, under His dominion; therefore, you should not go astray to serve idols from among the gods of other nations. This is the sense of the verse, "Not because you were greater than all the nations did God desire you and choose you . . ." It would have been proper for the Supreme King's people to be the most numerous, as it is written, "In the multitude of people is the king's glory" (Proverbs 14:28), and that He appoint [angels] over the other nations. But "you are the smallest"—yet He desired you and chose you (Nachmanides, ad loc.).

It was because of God's love for you . . . (Deuteronomy 7:8).

Commentary: [The Torah] only mentions this because one who knows that he has been chosen to be loved is prepared to suffer for the sake of his lover. The Israelites are more qualified for this than any other people. Thus, our Sages taught: "Three creatures are obdurate: among the nations, Israel . . ." (*Beitza* 25b), for Israel has stood beside God throughout their trials. [When challenged by the nations, Israel stubbornly declared,] "Either [permit us to live as] Jews, or [we shall submit to death at] the stake" (Nachmanides, ad loc.).

Suffering for Humanity

Who can believe what we have heard? Upon whom was God's hand revealed? He grew like a young plant before Him, like a root in a parched land, without form or beauty. We saw him, but he had no appearance that we should find him attractive.

Despised, rejected by humanity—a man of suffering, familiar with sickness, people averted their eyes from him. He was despised, and we considered him worthless. Yet he bore our sickness and endured our pain. We considered him diseased, smitten by God, tortured.

He was wounded because of our sins, crushed by our transgressions. Through his affliction we enjoyed tranquility; through his wounds we were healed. We strayed like sheep, each of us went his own way, and God visited upon him all of our sins (Isaiah 53:1–6).

Commentary: "Who can believe what we have heard?" Thus will the nations exclaim when they see Israel attain its destiny. "Upon whom was God's hand revealed?" Who would have thought that God's hand would be revealed upon such a despised nation? "He grew like a young plant before Him." Those who were formerly despised and exploited now arise like a young plant. Today's young plant grows up and becomes tomorrow's great tree; its roots reach into the earth; later it bears leaves and fruit and becomes a mighty cedar. Thus did Israel arise from "a parched land." Formerly, during their exile, Israel "lacked form or beauty. We saw him, but he had no appearance that we should find him attractive." His present appearance is completely differ-

122

ent. "Despised, rejected by humanity." This was his former condition. No people in the world suffered so much, nor endured such sickness. "People averted their eyes from him. He was despised and we considered him worthless." Previously, when the Creator concealed His face from them, Israel was despised and considered worthless. "Yet he bore our sickness." Now we see that Israel's belief in God is true. The sickness that we deserved, Israel bore. The suffering that we deserved, Israel endured. "We considered him diseased, smitten by God, tortured." When we would see Jews stricken with disease or beaten and tortured, we would say, "God brought this plague and this affliction upon them for not upholding His decrees and laws." However, "he was wounded because of our sins." The matter was not as we had imagined. Rather, because of our transgressions was Israel wounded [during its exile] among the nations. It cannot be said that the transgressions of the Jews were the cause [of their afflictions], because now we can see that they are exalted and elevated above all mankind. Certainly, they have followed God's decrees and laws. What caused them to be wounded and crushed? Our many sins. "Through his affliction, we enjoyed tranquility." The affliction Israel bore in accepting the yoke of God's sovereignty was the price of our tranquility. The Holy One, blessed be He, created one righteous nation in the world, which bore all the world's sins, so that the world could endure. "Through his wounds, we were healed." This has become a healing for us. "We strayed like sheep." The nations now admit to having followed false precepts and false doctrines[17] (MaHari Kara, ad loc.).

---

17. Note Jeremiah 16:19: "O God, my strength and stronghold, my refuge in times of trouble, nations will come to You from the ends of the earth and say, 'Our ancestors inherited falsehood, empty beliefs which contain no benefit.'"

All Nations Are Beloved

Although You love the nations, all of [God's] holy ones are in Your hand; they are subdued beneath Your feet, [for] he brought Your word (Deuteronomy 33:3).

Commentary: "Although You love the nations." With this You make known that all of humanity is precious to You. As the rabbis taught: "Beloved is man, who was created in the Divine image" (*Avos* 3:14). Nevertheless, "all [God's] holy ones are in Your hand." You declare that all [God's] holy ones—"the holy myriads" [who received] "the fiery religion" [as stated in the previous verse]—are in Your hand, as silver [in the hand] of the refiner. "They are subdued." They are broken, like one who has been reproved and prays with a broken spirit. "Beneath Your feet." That is, at Your footstool, Mount Sinai. "He brought Your word." This is the Torah which Moses commanded. They said to God, "Moses brought us Your word, the Torah which You commanded us to heed" (Rabbi Ovadyah Sforno, ad loc.).

And now, if you will diligently listen to My voice and observe My covenant, you shall be consecrated (*segula*) to Me from all the nations—for all the earth is Mine. And you shall be a kingdom of *Kohanim* (Priests) and a holy nation unto Me (Exodus 19:5–6).

Commentary: "You shall be consecrated to Me." Humanity as a whole is more precious to Me than the lower forms of existence, since man is the central figure in creation; as our Sages taught: "Beloved is man who was created in the Divine image" (*Avos* 3:14). However, the difference between [Jews and non-Jews] in the hierarchy of the universe is that, although "the entire earth belongs to Me," and the righteous of the nations are precious to Me without a doubt, [nevertheless] "you shall be a kingdom of *kohanim* (priests) unto Me." This is your distinction: you shall be a kingdom of *kohanim* (priests) to teach all of humanity, that "they all shall call upon the name of God to serve Him with a common accord" (Zephaniah 3:9). It also states, "And you shall be called the *kohanim* (priests) of God" (Isaiah 61:6), and, "For out of Zion shall the Torah come forth [and the word of God from Jerusalem]" (Isaiah 2:3). (Rabbi Ovadyah Sforno, ad loc.).

Between Heaven and Earth

We have often explained that Israel is foremost in the hierarchy of creation (*Bereishis Rabba* 1:4), and that once Israel has received Divine beneficence, it transfers this good to the nations who are beneath it. Thus the verse states, "I am in love, therefore God hears my voice" (Psalms 116:1). I am in love with God, which brings me close to Him. Because of this closeness, God hears my prayer. He bestows good upon me, and I, in turn, can share it with all mankind (Maharal of Prague, *Commentary on the Haggadah, Hallel*).

And I will make you into a great nation, and I will bless you, and I will make your name great: become a blessing (Genesis 12:2).

Commentary: The People of Abraham, in private and in public, follow one calling: to become a blessing. They dedicate themselves to the Divine purpose of bringing happiness to the world by serving as a model for all nations and to restore mankind to the pure spiritual status that Adam had possessed. [When this task has been completed,] God will grant His blessing of the renewal of life and the awakening and enlightenment of the nations, and the name of the People of Abraham shall shine forth (Rabbi Samson Raphael Hirsch, *Commentary on the Pentateuch*, ad loc.).

To be a prophet unto the nations did I appoint you . . . (Jeremiah 1:5).

Commentary: As the time was approaching—[Jeremiah] himself lived through it—for Israel to start on its path through the wilderness of the nations, every word of God directed through the prophet to Israel was at the same time related to humanity in general. Was not the later prophet Ezekiel simply called *ben adam*—"son of mankind"? From beginning to end, the words of the "Old Testament" know nothing of a "tribal God of the Jews," of a Divine Providence directed solely to Israel. From the beginning in Genesis, where the first Jew is introduced to history with the words "be thou a blessing," and, "through you all the families of the world shall be blessed" (Genesis 12:2, et seq.), to the last words of the Prophets, Israel is intimately bound up with all the families of the world. [This universal purpose is] on an equal plane with [Israel's] calling to be the "children of God" and to follow Him. To inspire [the other nations] and lead them to God constitutes its own historic mission as the priesthood of the human race (Rabbi Mendel Hirsch, ad loc.).

Hear, O mountains, God's contention, and you mighty foundations of the earth; for God has a dispute with His people, and with Israel will He contend (Micah 6:2).

Commentary: By being compared to "mountains" and "mighty foundations of the earth," Israel is reminded of their ideal calling to bring the consciousness of God to the rest of humanity. This realization is the true foundation of human happiness. Thus, the term "foundation" is applied to those whose task is to bring this about: Israel (Rabbi Mendel Hirsch, ad loc.).

Be astonished, O heavens, at this, and storm; devastate greatly, declares the Lord. For two evils have My people committed: they have forsaken Me, the Fount of Living Waters, to dig out for themselves cisterns, broken cisterns that do not hold water (Jeremiah 2:12–13).

Commentary: There is an intimate connection between nature and the calling of Israel to pave the way for all mankind to serve God. Nature itself cries out when Israel fails to perform its mission, and the attainment of this goal is pushed off into the distant future (Rabbi Mendel Hirsch, ad loc.).

Jethro's Wisdom

It is remarkable that Moses was instructed concerning the hierarchy of leadership by his Midianite father-in-law, Jethro. The reason for this was that God wanted to show that generation of Israelites and all their descendants that there are great Sages among other nations. As may be seen from the advice he gave Moses, Jethro was living proof that other nations possess men of great intellect and wisdom. Thus, the Torah makes known that the Jewish people were not chosen because of their intellectual superiority, but because of God's gratuitous kindness and His love for the Patriarchs.

This also sheds light on the opinion stated in the Talmud that Jethro came to Moses in the wilderness of Sinai prior to the Giving of the Torah (*Zevachim* 116a). Before He gave the Torah to Israel, God knew that there were greater Sages among other nations; nevertheless, God drew us near to Him and chose us. For this in particular we should gratefully praise God for His kindness. Also, according to the contrary opinion that Jethro arrived after the Giving of the Torah (op. cit.), this would explain why the Torah recounts Jethro's arrival beforehand. Only in this way would [the reason for God's choice] be apparent (Rabbi Chaim ibn Attar, *Ohr HaChaim* on Exodus 18:21).

In Their Merit

[God] does not gaze upon the transgression of Jacob, nor does He see iniquity in Israel (Numbers 23:21).

Commentary: Because of the two levels that characterize the Jewish people [indicated by the names "Jacob" and "Israel"], God does not punish the world for its evil or destroy the nations. "He does not gaze upon the transgression" of the world because of Jacob. [This name is derived from the Hebrew word for "heel." Thus, it denotes the Jewish people during their exile, when they are downtrodden.] Moreover, "He does not see iniquity" because of Israel. [The Hebrew word for iniquity can also mean exertion or strenuous effort. In other words,] God does not exert Himself, so to speak, with the burden of the world and its sustenance, or with those who are undeserving except for the sake of Israel. [This name is related to the Hebrew word for "ruler." Thus, it denotes the Jewish people when they live up to their spiritual ideal.] When Israel follows the path of the Torah and its commandments, God confers His beneficence upon the world and feeds and gratifies all nations together (Rabbi Chaim ibn Attar, *Ohr HaChaim*, ad loc.).

Why Israel Is Called "Adam"

I have always found it difficult to understand the statement of our Sages that whenever the Torah uses the term *adam* (man), it refers only to Israel (*Yevamos* 61a). [This statement in its context is part of a technical discussion concerning the laws of ritual impurity and has nothing to do with how Jews should perceive or treat non-Jews. The author of this essay is concerned with the indirect implications of this statement.] The Talmud also teaches that non-Jews possess the Divine image (*Avos* 3:14). However, the [former] statement might lead one to assume that they should be regarded as mere beasts. If this were the case, how could the Holy One, blessed be He, have declared, "You shall be My treasured people from all of the nations"? If all other nations are as mere beasts of the earth, this declaration would amount to saying, "You shall be My treasured people from all the animals and all the apes, whose appearance is like that of humans." All their actions, too, would be the actions of beasts, regarding which reward and punishment do not apply. This contradicts the rabbinic principle that righteous non-Jews deserve a place in the World to Come (*Sanhedrin* 105a).

If the holy words of our rabbis had not come to inform us of this [principle], we would have known it already through our own reason. For "God is righteous in all His ways, and merciful in all His deeds" (Psalms 145:17). [Therefore, it follows that He judges all people according to their potential for good or evil, and rewards them befittingly.]

We have seen how many righteous non-Jews not only recognize the Creator, believe in the Divine origin of the Torah, and treat the Jewish people with kindness, but also strive to benefit all of humanity. It is unthinkable that their good deeds go unrewarded in the World to Come, for the Holy One, blessed be He, does not withhold recompense from any creature. This reinforces our original question: Since [non-Jews were created in] the Divine image, and God, being "righteous and merciful in all His deeds," granted them a portion in the World to Come, why are they not called *adam*?

The medieval Talmudic scholars of France (*Baalei Tosefos*) in their glosses on the Talmudic passage cited above point out that the collective singular *ha-adam* (man), with the definite article, does include non-Jews. If non-Jews are not designated by the term *adam*, why should the definite article make a difference? Similarly, on the scriptural verse, "[The heavens are the heavens of the Lord,] and the earth He gave unto the children of man (*b'nei adam*)," the Talmud states that this includes non-Jews (*Gittin* 47b). If their ancestors were not called *adam*, how could they be called "children of man" (*b'nei adam*)? However, God enlightened my eyes to see the profundity of our Sages' dictum.

When the Jewish people were in Egypt, they and all other nations were like orphans without a father, dwelling together in darkness, ignorant of God. Not only did Pharaoh say, "I do not know God," but even Israel lacked any recognition of their Father in Heaven. [Thus, at the Burning Bush] Moses was compelled to inquire of the Holy One, blessed be He, "When they ask me, 'What is His name?' what shall I tell them?" (Exodus 3:13). And even later, when they crossed the Sea of Reeds, their faith was weak, and their hearts were still drawn to idolatry. The Talmud states concerning the verse, "They crossed the straits of the sea," that the idol of Micah crossed over with them (*Sanhedrin* 103b). This shows that their moral depravity and conduct was like that of the Egyptians, and they knew of no obligation to God, to their fellow men, or to themselves. All the more so was this true of the other nations.

God compelled them to acknowledge His existence and

providential hand through the plagues with which He afflicted Egypt. What is greater, He revealed Himself to them in a wondrous and awesome vision at Sinai, in a flame of fire that reached unto the heart of heaven. Through darkness, cloud, and thick cloud, He caused them to hear His commandments, decrees, and teachings, which include all human obligations. He subsequently instructed them in the orders of right conduct concerning the division of their camps and their cleanliness, their banners, signal trumpets, and holy vessels, etc., such that the entire reason for their success thenceforth was not known to them through their own power of intellect but through the [prophetic revelation of] the Holy One, blessed be He, Himself, in His glory.

However, while God was drawing Israel closer to their destiny, the rest of the world remained asleep, sunken in the depths of various abominations. All of their subsequent spiritual attainments were the result of their own efforts. Thus, it could be said that they "made" themselves. From then until now, many non-Jews drew waters of knowledge from the wellsprings of Israel's Torah. In the course of time they learned many ethical precepts as well as many principles of self-improvement; for, like the sunrise, the light of Divine Intellect dawned upon them very gradually. Only through time and great effort did they attain [their present level].

Thus it is that Israel and the other nations each possesses a unique advantage. The superiority of the nations over Israel is that, as a result of their free choice and by their own efforts, they made themselves. This is certainly an accomplishment that exceeds that of Israel, who, by Divine intervention, were coerced to attain their ultimate spiritual level. They have little with which to congratulate themselves in that God acted wondrously to uplift them. Throughout all their vicissitudes, the hand of God was upon them only in the merit of their ancestors.

Nevertheless, Israel, too, possesses a unique advantage over the other nations. All that the nations apprehended was only through their own intellect. However, there are many commandments that are far beyond the grasp of mortal intellect. Thus, [even the other nations that believe in the Divine origin of the Torah] do not perform all of the biblical decrees that are not comprehensible—they will be so only at the end of days, when "God will pour forth His Spirit upon all flesh." Also, since all that they grasped was only through mortal intellect, those among them who neglected to open their eyes still remain sunken in their former abominations, serving mute idols and sacrificing their children to demons, like their ancestors from time immemorial. For "they knew not God, and His Torah they did not recognize." Not so Israel. They observe all the statutes of the Torah, even those beyond mortal intellect. The entire nation, from the least to the greatest, has faith in God, having been nurtured on the Divine Torah from their infancy; for God forced open their eyes to recognize the path of life.

Thus, the verse states, "This nation I formed for Myself . . ." (Isaiah 43:21). That is, God made them, as it is written, "He made us, and we belong to Him" (Psalms 100:3). "They shall declare My praise" (Isaiah 43:21). "It is befitting that they praise Me." However, the Jewish people do not praise themselves. When it says, "Your people are all righteous; they shall inherit the land forever," they do not attribute this to their own efforts, but only because [God declared,] "They are the first-fruits of My planting. I Myself formed them; yea, even made them. . . . The work of My hands, in which I take pride" (Isaiah 43:7, 60:21).

Accordingly, in their lofty status and ultimate spiritual perfection, Israel is comparable to Adam, the first man. Ordinarily a child is born lacking wisdom, until through time, study, and innate ability it develops into a mature human being. This was not the case with Adam, who was born fully grown and developed (*Rosh Hashanah* 11a). As soon as the breath of life was blown into him, Adam was able to speak with intellect and wisdom, cognizant of his duties. Like Adam, Israel was the recipient of Divine commandments, having been prepared for this by the Holy One, blessed be He.

[As a rule,] whenever the circumstances and deeds of a son are comparable to those of his father, [the Torah] mentions them in the name of the father. For example, the verse states, "Thus shall Aaron approach the Holy of Holies," meaning the *Kohen Gadol* (High Priest), who must be a descendant of Aaron. Similarly, the verse states, "That My covenant may be with Levi" (Malachi 2:4), meaning all of his descendants. It states, "And they shall seek the Lord, their God, and David, their king" (Hosea 3:5), meaning the king, who shall be of Davidic lineage. Likewise, "And My servant, David, shall be king over them" (Ezekiel 37:24) refers to the Messianic King, who must be his descendant. Our holy Matriarchs, too, were called by the name of Israel, their father. This was not only because "his bed was perfect" [i.e., all of his children were righteous], but also because all that happened to the Patriarch Israel—his endurance of persecution and misfortune from youth until old age—happened to them. As the verse states, "'Many times have they afflicted me since my youth,' let Israel now declare" (Psalms 129:1), [meaning all those who are called by the name "Israel"].

From this point of view, it would be inappropriate to call all people *adam*. Adam was so named because he was formed of the earth (Hebrew: *adamah*), whereas the rest of his descendants were born of flesh and blood. [That is, he was formed directly by God; the rest of mankind was formed through natural procreation.] Israel alone deserves to be called by this name—not because of their greater honor, but because, like Adam, all that happened to them, as well as their spiritual perfection, was the doing of the Holy One, blessed be He, Himself, and not primarily the result of their own endeavor.

Therefore, wherever the Torah uses the term *adam* (man), it means Israel exclusively. The Talmud explains that a different term for man—*ish*—refers to all mankind. Thus, the verse states, "From each person (*ish*) voluntary offerings are accepted," meaning to include members of other nations. However, the name *adam* would not befit them, for the exceedingly demanding task of non-Jews has been to fulfill their potential through their own efforts. [In this sense] they are unlike Adam, the first man.

However, wherever Scripture uses the term "children of Adam," it includes the nations of the world, for we are all his descendants. And, certainly, wherever the term *adam* is written with the definite article, it does not refer to the first man. He is called by his proper name: Adam. No proper name requires the definite article—one does not say, "the Abraham," "the Isaac," or "the Israel." Thus, it would be improper to refer to the first man as "the Adam." Clearly, in this case the meaning is different. *Ha-adam* (with the definite article) refers to all mankind; for we are all rational beings who possess the Divine image, Jews and non-Jews alike.

In conclusion, the statement that "only Israel may be properly called *adam*" is not such high praise; rather, it attests that not by their own efforts did the Jewish people remove the thick covering of their spiritually blocked hearts, but only because they were like "clay in the hands of the Former," the Holy One, blessed be He (Rabbi Yisrael Lifshutz, *Tiferes Yisrael* (*Boaz*) on *Avos* 3:14, abridged).

Dedication to God

The highest mission of all other nations is to preserve their own national existence. However, the purpose of the Jewish people is extrinsic, for it is a nation not unto itself but unto God. It must place itself, in every possible area of relationship, in every aspect of its individual, family, and public life, prepared and ready for whatever purpose or task God indicates. Hence, it must remove itself from anything that would mitigate against these purposes. "For you are a holy people unto the Lord, your God . . ."[18]

The designation "a treasured people . . . from all the nations" means that the Jewish people belong to no other power and must develop exclusively on the basis of belonging to God. Thus, the phrase "from all the nations" underscores their condition of chosenness. Or, alternately, the phrase could be rendered "more than all the nations," meaning that what God has done for the Jewish people gives Him a greater right over them (so to speak) than over all other nations (Rabbi Samson Raphael Hirsch, *Commentary on the Torah*, Deuteronomy 7:6).

---

18. The Hebrew word *kadosh* (holy) also denotes a committed relationship that excludes other relationships. Thus, in Talmudic law, marriage is designated by the related term *kiddushin*. It is in this sense that the giving of the Torah to the Israel at Mount Sinai is compared to a wedding. The entire Jewish people formally dedicated themselves to God alone and renounced idolatry.

Higher than Mind

For we are called *am segula*—a treasured nation. This is like a *segula* (charm) used for healing. Even though nature does not dictate that it should bring about healing, nevertheless this thing is propitious for curing illness. It is supernatural, beyond the comprehension of the mortal mind. Similarly, God took us to be His "treasured nation," even though the mortal mind cannot comprehend all this—how and why one nation was picked from other nations. [Therefore, the Midrash states that] during the splitting of the Red Sea, the Divine Attribute of Justice accused: "These are idol-worshipers [and so are these] . . ." (*Shemos Rabba* 21:7). Nevertheless, the Holy One, blessed be He, chose us to be a holy nation.

This phenomenon is like a *segula*, higher than nature, higher than human intellect. It is part of Transcendent Intellect. [Only] someone who merits [to grasp] Transcendent Intellect, to give birth to it and internalize it, will merit to understand the *segula*—the incomprehensible. Certainly, it is fitting to reveal this *segula* to the *am segula* (treasured nation) (Rabbi Nachman of Breslov, *Likkutei Moharan* I, 21:9).

Brotherhood of Mankind

The Torah calls Israel *am segula*—a treasured nation. However, this does not imply, as some have mistakenly assumed, that Israel has a monopoly on God's love and favor. On the contrary, it proclaims that God has the sole and exclusive claim to the Jewish people's devotion and service, and that Israel may not worship any other being. Israel's most cherished ideal is that of the universal brotherhood of mankind. Almost every page of our prayers refers to the hastening of this end.

Everyone is helping to raise up a great edifice, Divinely ordained for the benefit of humanity. To this end are dedicated all the nations that exist or have ever existed on the face of the earth, whether in the east or the west, the north or the south, each with its own entrance and exit from the stage of history, each with its successes and failures, its virtues and vices, its wisdom and folly, its rise and its fall—with whatever it leaves to posterity as the sum total of its existence.

All of these efforts and accomplishments are the building blocks contributed by the various nations to the common edifice of history; all take part in carrying out the plan of the same One God (Rabbi Samson Raphael Hirsch, *The Nineteen Letters*, Letter 15).

Israel is holy unto God; the first of the fruits of His planting . . . (Jeremiah 1:3).

Commentary: [The verse suggests that both Israel and the other nations of the world are considered "fruits of His planting."] The whole of mankind is summoned to a filial relationship with God. Throughout humanity, God has planted the seed of a perfected human race in every soul. He waits for this seed to sprout, and furthers its growth by the destiny He ordains. Israel is only the first fruit, the first reaping that matures for Him on the human soil. We see again how every thought of any exclusiveness of Israel's relationship to God is refuted (Rabbi Mendel Hirsch, ad loc.).

Unity in Diversity

"God said unto [Jacob]: I am God, the All-Sufficing. Be fruitful and multiply; a nation and a community of nations shall come into existence from you" (Genesis 35:11). The nation that is to descend from him is to represent one entity to the outside world, but internally it is to be a multiplicity of elements united into one. Each tribe is to represent an ethnic individuality in its own right. The nation of Jacob, which as "Israel" is to demonstrate to the other nations the power of God triumphantly pervading and shaping all of mankind, should not present a one-sided image. As a model nation, it should reflect the greatest possibility of national characteristics in microcosm. In its tribes it should represent variously the warrior nation, the merchant nation, the agricultural nation, the nation of scholars, etc. In this manner it will become clear to all the world that the consecration of human life to the covenant with the Law of God does not demand occupational restrictions or depend on specific ethnic characteristics, but that all mankind in all its multiplicity is capable of accepting the concept of monotheism taught by Israel, and of fashioning the multiplicity of human and national individualities into one united kingdom of God (Rabbi Samson Raphael Hirsch, *Commentary on the Pentateuch*, ad loc.).

Dedication to Mankind

I, I am your Comforter. Who are you to fear mortal man, or the son of a human being who is given unto the grass? . . . For I have placed My words in your mouth, and in the shadow of My hand I have covered you—to plant Heaven and to establish the earth's foundation and to say unto Zion: You are My people (Isaiah 51:12, 16).

Commentary: God made Israel the bearer of His word and sent it to mankind with the teaching that all men are God's children, regardless of race or religion, with the practice of justice and love toward all without exception, and with the Torah of the One God, who does not wish His human children to go to ruin in the slime of immorality or in the streams of blood spilt in the glorification of power and violence. He knew that His people, in upholding this teaching in the midst of a world that worshiped power and might, would be exposed to bitter hatred and enmity. Nevertheless, [Israel was commanded] to live by morality, kindness, and truth where otherwise profitability, expedience, and gain were the deciding factors, and success was revered above all. [At the same time, God assured Israel, "I, I am your Comforter. Who are you to fear mortal man? . . ." In other words,] "When I sent you out on this dangerous mission I equipped you beforehand with My special protection" (Rabbi Mendel Hirsch, ad loc.).

The purpose of Israel has always been to serve as a "vessel that contains blessing" and goodness for all mankind, inasmuch as it was prepared for this from its birth. Therefore, even when [Israel] sins, turning aside from the path of God, it does so only because it has been misled to think that it will actually fulfill its spiritual mission by repudiating the Lord, its God. However, its true motivation is [nevertheless] to be a blessing unto all who are created in the Divine image and to delight in bringing benefit and happiness to all mankind, [a calling] that is permanently fixed in the innermost depths of its soul (Rabbi Avraham Yitzchak Kook, *Ein Ayah, Berachos* II:115).

When Abraham was circumcised and thus became a convert, the Chosen People was founded. However, this concept of chosenness was based on a goal, a task, and a burden, rather than on privileges, and it is this idea that distinguishes Jewish nationalism from the concept of nationalism that prevails among other peoples. Jewish nationalism is based on a dedication to all mankind. This theme is particularly evident in our prayer on the Days of Awe, in which we pray for the day when "all creatures will bow before You and form one group to do Your will with a full heart," and in the very next paragraph we beseech God: "Grant honor to Your people . . . joy to Your land, and exaltation to Your city." This is why, concurrently with his circumcision, Abraham acquired a new name. In place of the name Abram, which has only local significance, the name Abraham, which has universal significance, was conferred upon him.[19] This symbolizes the Jewish nation's duty to act as the nucleus that is to preserve all mankind. Without a representative dedicated to the concept of suffering with commitment, mankind as a whole could not survive (Rabbi Ahron Soloveichik, *The Warmth and The Light*, "Nationalism and Universalism").

---

19. Genesis 17:5. The verse states that "Abraham" connotes his role as *av hamon goyim*—"father of many nations."

And you shall say to Pharaoh: Thus says God, "Israel is My son, My firstborn" (Exodus 4:22).

Commentary: All the people of the world, in view of the perfect future, are children of God inasmuch as in the end they will all recognize the sovereignty of God. Israel is and will always remain the eldest son of God simply because Israel is the pioneer in paving the road for the march of God through the avenues of the human race. Yet all people will equally dedicate themselves to the moral values that are inherent in the ethical attributes of God. The saying of Rabbi Akiva, "Beloved is Man, who was created in the image of God; it is by special distinction that he was created in the image of God" (*Avos* 3:14), implies that every human being, regardless of religion, race, origin, or creed is endowed with Divine dignity. Consequently, all people are to be treated with equal respect and dignity (Rabbi Ahron Soloveichik, *Logic of the Heart, Logic of the Mind*, "Civil Rights and the Dignity of Man").

3

The Messianic Vision

INTRODUCTION

The universalism of the Torah is most fully expressed by the Messianic vision of the ancient prophets of Israel. This vision attests to the unity of all creation and to life's ultimate purpose. Human existence is not merely an endless cycle of birth and death, success and failure, gratification and disappointment. Whether we understand it or not, everything that happens is part of the Divine plan—and the goal of that plan is for all of humanity to live in a world without strife or want, in which the "knowledge of God" will be our foremost pursuit. This period of lasting world peace and enlightenment is the Messianic era.

Modern art and literature is haunted by a sense of meaninglessness and cosmic indifference. In truth, these feelings characterize the human experience whenever people lose their moral and spiritual moorings. The revelations of the Messianic era will not only provide the final antidote for this pervasive existential distress, but its *tikkun* (rectification). That is, everything we have experienced hitherto—every facet of the human experience—will become a vessel for enlightenment. Chasidic master Rabbi

145

Nachman of Breslov once remarked that the Messiah will explain everything that happened to us on every day of our lives.[1] The true meaning of every detail of history and its place in the Divine plan will be revealed. Moreover, human nature will no longer be ruled by selfishness, passion, and aggression. Corresponding to the perception of God's Oneness will be a profound sense of the unity of life; thus, our hearts will be full of compassion and respect for one another and for all that exists. As the verse states: "A new heart I will give you, as well, and a new spirit I will put in you; I will take away the heart of stone from your flesh, and I will give you a heart of flesh" (Ezekiel 36:26).

The subject of the Messiah is beyond the scope of this book. Yet the various issues presented here are very much bound up with this fundamental component of Jewish belief. Therefore, we have included some of the key prophecies concerning the Messianic era, together with their traditional interpretations, as they touch upon the theme of universalism. Since many readers may be unfamiliar with the larger context of these prophecies, we have also attempted to give a brief overview of the Messianic idea in rabbinic Judaism.

The word "Messiah" in its original Hebrew (*mashiach*) means "anointed." The ancient kings of Israel were anointed with oil by the prophet of the generation. This act of anointing designated a particular individual as king.[2] In a deeper sense, however, anointing is an act of spiritual empowerment. The pure oil poured upon the head of the king symbolizes Divine Wisdom,

1. *Sippurei Ma'asios, Ma'aseh* 10 (*Burgher V'Ani*), *Sichos Achar HaMa'aseh.* Citing this teaching, Rabbi Gedaliah Kenig explains that the Messiah will be granted the knowledge of everything that ever happened, for he alone will be able to bring about the world's ultimate *tikkun* (rectification); see *Chayei Nefesh*, chap. 21, pp. 33–34.

2. I Samuel 9:16, 10:1, 16:3, 16:12–13; *Tosefta, Sanhedrin* 3:2; *Sifri* and Ramban on Deuteronomy 17:15; *Mishneh Torah, Sanhedrin* 5:1; ibid., *Melachim* 1:3.

which is conferred by an act of grace.[3] The greatest wisdom will
be given to the greatest king: the Messiah. Thus, the verse states
that he will be "full of wisdom and understanding, counsel and
might, knowledge and fear of God" (Isaiah 11:2).[4] Like his
forebear, King David, the Messiah is both a ruler and prophet.[5]
He is the ultimate political leader as well as the ultimate Sage and
spiritual teacher. In fact, it is his spiritual stature that establishes
his sovereignty—not brute force.[6]

One of the Messiah's distinguishing characteristics will be his
self-effacement. (In Chasidic teachings, this is called bitul ha-yesh,
or, simply, bitul.) Just as the Torah describes Moses as the "humblest
man in the world" (Numbers 12:3), so does the Messiah embody
this trait. Indeed, the Kabbalah states that the Messiah will
possess the soul of Moses.[7] Due to his attainment of bitul, the

---

3. See Rabbi Menachem M. Schneerson of Lubavitch, On the Essence of
Chassidus, chap. 7, citing Imrei Binah, Sha'ar HaKrias Shema, chap. 54, 56;
Torah Ohr 39a; Likkutei Torah, Naso 27d. Also note Likkutei Halachos, Birkas
HaRei'ach 3:8 and 4:5.

4. Also note Arba Me'os Shekel Kesef of the Ari z"l, p. 241, citing Zohar,
Shemos 7b. There Rabbi Chaim Vital states that the Messiah will be a righteous
person who will advance from level to level until the moment arrives for the
final redemption. Then he will be granted "the soul of souls" from the Garden
of Eden and gain the power of prophecy, thus to complete his mission.

5. Ibn Ezra, Radak on Isaiah 11:1; Sanhedrin 98b; Eichah Rabbah 1:51.

6. Likkutei Halachos, Yom Tov 5:9; Rabbi Levi Yitzhak Bender, Si'ach Sarfei
Kodesh II, 1:67; this is similar to the prophecy concerning Israel's return from
Babylonian captivity; cf. Mahari Kara, Radak, Metzudas Tzion on Zechariah
4:6.

7. "That which was shall be" (Ecclesiastes 1:9). In Hebrew, the initial letters
of the first three words of this verse spell the name Moses (Moshe), as stated
in Tikkunei Zohar, Tikkun 69, 111b; Zohar II, 120a. The Messiah is compared
to both David and Moses, since each biblical figure personifies one of the
Messiah's attributes. In general, Moses represents Torah and prophecy, whereas
David represents prayer; see Likkutei Halachos, Rosh Chodesh 5:6–7; ibid.,
Nefilas Apayim 4:24; ibid., Yayin Nesech 3:6. Also, there will be a "Messiah son
of Joseph" who dies in battle, as discussed in Sukkah 52a, based on Zechariah
12:10–14; see Emunos V'De'os 8:5; Nachmanides on Exodus 17:10; Maharal,
Netzach Yisrael 36; Pri Eitz Chaim, Sha'ar HaAmidah (Birkas Tishkon); Ohr

Messiah is able to transcend his ordinary human limitations and become a vehicle for Divine Intellect.[8] Thus, he rules with the greatest wisdom. His extreme humility also makes him capable of relating to every human being. When there is no "self," there is no barrier to anyone else. Then it is possible to express true compassion.[9]

This is not to suggest that the Messiah will refrain from judging evil-doers. He will see through sham and hypocracy, intuitively knowing a person's thoughts and former deeds (*Sanhedrin* 93b). The Prophet Isaiah states: "[The Messiah] will not judge by what his eyes see or decide by what his ears hear. He will judge the poor righteously. He will smite the tyrant with the rod of his mouth and slay the wicked with the breath of his lips" (Isaiah 11:3–4).[10] Nevertheless, his primary task is not to punish or exact vengeance but to bring peace. Thus, the Talmud asserts: "When the Messiah is revealed to Israel, his first task will be to

---

HaChaim on Numbers 24:17 and Leviticus 14:9; *Sh'nei Luchos HaBris, Beis David* 1:37b. Some authorities understand this symbolically: the Messiah son of Joseph is not an individual but personifies the Sages of each generation who exert themselves to the point of self-sacrifice in order to bring others back to God. Note Rabbi Menachem Kasher's *HaTekufah HaGedolah*, citing *Kol HaTor* from the school of the Vilna Gaon; Rabbi Shmuel Horowitz's *Tzion Ham'tzuyenes* (Breslov), p. 42 (sec. 58), citing *Sichos V'Sippurim* of Rabbi Avraham Ben Nachman Chazan. Interestingly, the latter text (sec. 78, p. 58) points out that the final letters of the Hebrew names for Moses, David, and Joseph spell the word "redeem."

8. *Kiddushas Levi, Eikev*, on *Avos* 2:5; *Likkutei Moharan* I:79; also note *Biur HaLikkutim* on *Likkutei Moharan* I:20, sec. 7, 8; *Likkutei Halachos, Birkas HaRei'ach* 3:8.

9. Concerning the spiritual level of the Messiah, see *On the Essence of Chassidus*, chap. 5–6, especially note 41; *Zohar* II, 7b–8b, with the commentary *Matok Mid'vash; Zohar HaRakiah, Shemos* 56b. Also note the teaching of the Baal Shem Tov cited in *Ma'or Einaim, Pinchas*, that the soul of the Messiah includes all souls; similarly, note the Ari z"l in *Eitz Chaim, Sha'ar* 42; *Sha'ar HaPesukim* 2:3, et al.

10. However, note *Likkutei Halachos, Hashkamas HaBoker* 1:12, that tempering strict justice with mercy actually brings the Messiah, for he personifies this balance of opposites.

establish peace. As it is written, 'How beautiful upon the mountains are the feet of the messenger who announces peace.'"[11] War and all forms of strife will cease to exist—particularly the strife of conflicting desires and emotions—and all mankind will turn to beneficial pursuits. Foremost among them will be the quest for knowledge of God. As the verse states: "And it shall come to pass afterward that I shall pour out My spirit on all flesh, and your sons and daughters shall prophecy; your elders shall dream dreams, your young men shall see visions; and also upon the servants and handmaids of those days shall I pour out My spirit" (Joel 3:1–2).

The *Zohar*, one of the classic texts of the Kabbalah, states that the miracles of the Messianic era will be greater than those of the Exodus from Egypt.[12] Wealth will be available to all in abundance—but the craving for wealth will cease to exist.[13] Food and drink will no longer require preparation, but will be produced ready for consumption.[14] Yet at that time, man will be content with the simplest sustenance.[15] The Messiah will be the catalyst for a mode of existence we can barely imagine. Moreover, as a human being, he will possess every manner of perfection. One of the names of the Messiah is *Peleh Yo'etz*—Wonderous Advisor—which indicates the miraculous nature of his wisdom and perception.[16] Nevertheless, he will be a mortal human being, born of human parents. For all his spiritual attainments, he is never deified, nor is he considered an object of worship. God

---

11. *Derech Eretz Zuta, Perek HaShalom*, citing Isaiah 52:7.
12. *Zohar* I, 261b; ibid., II, 9a, citing Micah 7:15: "Like during your exodus from the Land of Egypt, I will show you wonders."
13. *Baba Basra* 75a.
14. Joel 4:18; Amos 9:13; also note *Shabbos* 30b.
15. Rashi, Metzudas David, et al. on Isaiah 30:20.
16. Isaiah 9:5, according to *Likkutei Halachos, Eiruvei Techumin* 5:22: However, most commentators interpret *Peleh Yo'etz* as a Divine name and only the last name in the verse, "Prince of Peace," in reference to the Messiah.

alone is the source of all blessing—indeed, of all existence—and the Messiah is but an instrument of the Divine will.[17]

There are a number of key tasks that the Messiah will accomplish. The first is the redemption of the Jewish people and their return to the Holy Land. Throughout history, the Jewish people have endured untold suffering for the sake of their faith. Moreover, Israel is the medium through which God's teachings are imparted to all humanity. Therefore, the redemption of Israel will be the Messiah's first priority. He will also restore kingship to the House of David,[18] oversee the rebuilding of Jerusalem and the Third Holy Temple,[19] and reestablish the Sanhedrin—the religious supreme court and legislature of Jewish people. (This court is empowered to formally recognize the Messiah as king of Israel.)[20] After completing the rebuilding of the Holy Temple, he will renew the Temple service as it will pertain to the Messianic era.[21]

The Messiah's main task, however, is to bring the entire world

---

17. *Mishneh Torah, Avodas Kochavim* 2:1; ibid., *Melachim* 11:3; ibid., *Teshuvah* 3:7 (*Kesef Mishneh, Lechem Mishneh*, ad loc.). Also note *Nefesh HaChaim* 3:9 citing *Sanhedrin* 93a, *Bereishis Rabba* 96:6, and *Tanchuma, Vayechi* 3, that even worshiping a true prophet is an act of idolatry.

18. *Mishneh Torah, Melachim* 11:1.

19. There is a dispute as to whether the Messiah will rebuild the Holy Temple or whether it will appear on its site by an act of God. Maimonides takes the former position in his *Mishneh Torah, Melachim* 11:1, 4, based on the Jerusalem Talmud, *Megillah* 1:11; *Vayikra Rabbah* 9:6; and *Bamidbar Rabbah* 13:2. Rashi takes the latter in his glosses on *Sukkah* 41a and *Rosh Hashanah* 30a, based on *Tanchumah, Pekudei* 11, et al. This is also the view of the Kabbalah in *Zohar, Bereishis* 28a. Various later authorities attempt to resolve this contradiction.

20. Maimonides, *Mishneh Torah, Sanhedrin* 5:1; *Pirush al HaMishna, Sanhedrin* 1:3.

21. *Mishneh Torah, Melachim* 11:1. The only private sacrifices to be offered in those times will be the Thanksgiving Offering (*Korban Toda'ah*). Since man's heart will be pure, the desire to sin will no longer exist, and the Sin Offering (*Korban Chata'as*) will be unnecessary, as is discussed in *Sh'nei Luchos HaBris, Beis David* 1:37a; also note *Sefer HaMidos, Emes* I:8. Similarly, the only prayers

to return to God and His teachings.[22] In this way, God's absolute sovereignty will be known and established, and His beneficence will be shared by all (Zechariah 14:9). The Messiah will be sought out by all nations, and Jerusalem will become the spiritual capital of the world. The Jewish people will attain lofty spiritual levels, commensurate with their efforts throughout their long and bitter exile, and they will be regarded as the teachers of mankind.[23] Then the prophecy will be fulfilled: "I will imbue all people with a pure speech, that they may call upon the name of God and serve Him with a common accord" (Zephaniah 3:9).

How will we be able to recognize the Messiah? One would think that the climatic events preceding his advent would remove all doubt.[24] But evidently there will be a period in which the identity of the Messiah is unclear. Therefore, Maimonides states: "If there arises a ruler from the House of David who is immersed in the Torah and its commandments like David his ancestor— following both the Written Torah and the Oral Torah—and he leads Israel back to the Torah, strengthening the observance of its laws, and fighting God's battles, then we may presume that he is the Messiah. If he is successful in rebuilding the Temple on its original site and gathering the dispersed of Israel, then his

---

will be those of thanksgiving and praise. See *Eitz Yosef* on *Vayikra Rabbah* 9:17; Rabbi Aharon of Zelichov's *Kesser Shem Tov* 81.

22. *Mishneh Torah, Teshuvah* 9:2; ibid., *Melachim* 11:4.

23. Jeremiah 3:17; Zechariah 8:22–23; Isaiah 2:2–4; Micah 4:1–3; *Shemos Rabbah* 23:10; *Avos of Rabbi Nathan* 35:9; *Yalkut Shimoni* on Isaiah 499; Malbim on Isaiah 24:23.

24. The period of moral decline and massive social upheaval preceding the advent of the Messiah is called the *Chevlei Mashiach*—the "Birthpangs of the Messiah." See *Sanhedrin* 97a–98b; *Sotah* 49b; *Derech Eretz Zuta* 10; *Midrash Tanchuma, Noach* 3; *Zohar* III, 67b, 124b, 125b (*Rayah Mehemnah*), 153a; Maharal, *Netzach Yisrael* 36; *Sichos HaRan* 35, 220. Also note the prophecies in Daniel 12:10, Isaiah 59:15, et al. Concerning the apocalyptic war of Gog, king of Magog, see Ezekiel 38–39; *Berachos* 7b; *Sanhedrin* 95b; *Shabbos* 118a (end); *Midrash Tehillim* 11:5; Radak on Zechariah 14:1, et al.

identity as the Messiah is beyond doubt. He will then perfect the entire world and bring all men to serve God in unity."[25]

SOURCES

And it shall come to pass at the end of days that the mountain of God's House shall be established above the peaks and raised up above the heights, and all the nations shall flow to it. And many peoples shall say, "Come, and let us go up to the mountain of God, to the House of the God of Jacob; and He will teach us of His ways, and we shall go in His paths. For Torah shall go forth from Zion, and the word of God from Jerusalem." And he shall judge the nations and reprove many peoples; and they shall beat their swords into ploughshares and their spears into pruning-hooks; nation shall not raise the sword against nation, neither shall they learn war anymore (Isaiah 2:2–4).

Commentary: "For the Torah shall go forth from Zion." These are the words of the prophet, not those of the nations. It is as if he asks, "Why do the nations say, 'Come, let us go up, and He will teach us His ways'? [The next verse answers:] "For Torah shall go forth from Zion" to all the nations. The teacher will be the Messianic King, concerning whom it states, "And he shall judge the nations." If there is a dispute between one nation and another, they shall bring their case before the Messianic King, who will rule over all the world. He will "reprove them" by telling the oppressor, "Make aright the injustice you have done to the other disputant." Thus, there will be no war between nations. He will make peace between them, and, since they will no longer need their weapons of war, they will beat them down and make from them farm implements (Rabbi David Kimchi, ad loc.).

---

25. *Mishneh Torah, Melachim* 11:4.

House of Jacob, come, let us walk in the light of God (Isaiah 2:5).

Commentary: This refers to the Torah of God, which is "a light for their way" (paraphrase of Psalms 119:105). The verse is related to the previous theme [i.e., the coming of the Messiah and the establishment of world peace]. The prophet says to Israel, "The nations who are not descendants of Jacob are destined to renounce their empty beliefs and to say to one another, 'Come, let us walk in the light of God.' How much more so is it incumbent upon you, who are the descendants of Jacob, to prepare yourselves for this by renouncing your evil ways" (MaHari Kara, ad loc.).

The wolf will lie down with the lamb, and the leopard will lie down with the kid. The calf, the young lion, and the fattened ox will [flock] together, and a young child will lead them. The heifer and the bear will graze together, their young will lie down together, and the lion will eat straw like the cow. A suckling babe will play at a viper's hole, and an infant will stretch his hand over an adder's den. They will do no harm or damage in all My holy mountain, for the earth shall be full of the knowledge of God, as the water covers the sea (Isaiah 11:6–9).

Commentary: "The wolf will lie down with the lamb." All this may be understood allegorically. The wolf, leopard, bear, and lion represent the wicked who exploit and rob those weaker than themselves, like predatory animals [that attack] their prey. The lamb, calf, heifer and kid represent the meek of the earth. In the Messianic era there will be peace on earth, and people will no longer do evil to one another, as [this passage concludes], "They will do no harm or damage in all My holy mountain" (Rabbi David Kimchi, ad loc.).

Incline your ears and come to Me; listen, and your souls shall live! I will make an eternal covenant with you, enduring as My kindness to David. Yea, I have made him a witness unto the nations, a master and law-giver to the peoples. Yea, a nation you had not known you will call, and a nation who knew not of you shall come running, for the sake of the Lord your God, and the Holy One of Israel Who has glorified you (Isaiah 55:3–5).

Commentary 1:   "Enduring as My kindness to David." This alludes to the Messiah, who is named after [his forebear] David. Thus, it is written of [the Messiah], "And David, My servant, shall be a prince unto them forever" (Ezekiel 37:25). Just as My kindness to David endures, so shall My covenant with you endure. The verse also mentions David, for he will be the teacher of all the nations; as it is written, "And he shall judge the nations and reprove many peoples" (Isaiah 2:4). "A nation you did not know." This refers to the Jewish people who live far from the land of Israel. I will call them, and they shall come before you, despite the fact that until today, you did not know them, and they did not know you. When they hear of the wonders that God performed for you, they will fear you and run to perform your service, according to your command. And who gave you this glory? "The Lord, your God, [the Holy One of Israel]" (Rabbi David Kimchi, ad loc.).

Commentary 2:   "Listen, and your souls shall live." Listen to Me, and merit to return to life during the Messianic era. "I will make an eternal covenant with you." I will make a covenant of love with you that will last forever. "Enduring as My kindness to David." This covenant will endure like the promise I made to David that kingship will never cease from his lineage. "Behold, I have appointed him as a witness to the nations." Verily, I have made David a witness and a proof before the nations. His dominion, which continues through his seed, will prove to the world that God's promise is trustworthy. "A ruler and a law-giver to the peoples." The Messiah, who will come from the seed of David, will be a ruler, and, as such, will command the nations concerning their actions (*Metzudas David*, ad loc.).

∾

Thus spoke God, the Lord of Hosts: It shall yet come to pass that nations shall come, and the inhabitants of many cities, and the dwellers of one shall go to the other, saying, "Let us go beseech God and pray to the Lord of Hosts; I will go, too." And many peoples and mighty nations shall come to seek the Lord of Hosts in Jerusalem and to entreat Him. Thus said God, the Lord of Hosts: In those days it shall come to pass that ten men from the peoples of every tongue shall take hold of the garment of a Jewish man, saying, "We shall come with you, for we have heard that the Lord is with you" (Zechariah 8:20–23).

Commentary: This prophecy concerns the End of Days, when all nations of the world will acknowledge the true faith. This will take place in two stages. As the time of the Messianic Redemption draws near, all nations will recognize the holiness of Jerusalem, each one according to its own religion, and they will go there to pray to God. Since over the centuries monotheism had become widely disseminated through Christianity and Islam, [many nations] will consider Jerusalem to be God's city, and go there to pray. They will begin to "entreat God, the Lord of Hosts," i.e., to inquire into matters of faith. The Jewish people will still seem inferior in their eyes, and they will not ask them about their beliefs; nevertheless, the focal point of their spiritual search will be Jerusalem. The second part of [Zechariah's] prophecy describes how at the time of the Redemption itself the other nations will begin to accept the faith of Israel and to recognize the holiness of the Torah. When they see the *tzitzis* (ritual fringes) on a man's garment, they will know that he is a Jew. Having recognized that God is with Israel, they will go to Jerusalem together with the Jew in order to study the precepts and faith of Judaism (Rabbi Meir Leib Malbim, ad loc.).

∾

For the eyes of mankind will turn to God and to all the tribes of Israel (Zechariah 9:1).

Commentary: A time will come when all of humanity will search for God and therefore turn to the people of Israel for spiritual guidance (Rabbi David Kimchi, ad loc.).

And God will rule over all the earth; on that day God shall be One and His name shall be One (Zechariah 14:9).

Commentary 1: The verse means that all nations will accept God and believe in Him. They will no longer worship the forces of nature, not even to the extent of believing in intermediaries (*Metzudas David*, ad loc.).

Commentary 2: People have many ways of referring to God, according to their perceptions of His deeds, etc. However, "on that day God shall be One, and God's name will be One." Since God's essence will be revealed to all, he will be called by just one name (Rabbi David Kimchi, ad loc.).

God will wipe away the tears from all faces (Isaiah 25:8).

Midrash: Rabbi Yehoshua Ben Levi taught: This means from the faces of non-Jews as well (*Bereishis Rabba* 26:2).

To the Chief Musician, a psalm of the sons of Korach. May all the nations clap hands [and] sing to God with the voice of joyous song. For the Supreme Being is awesome, a great King over all the earth. He subdues people under us, and nations under our feet. He has chosen for us His inheritance, the pride of Jacob, the place that He loves, *sela*. The Lord has ascended with a blast; God, with the sound of the ram's horn. Sing praises to the Lord, sing praises; sing praises to our King, sing praises. For God is King of all the earth; sing praises, O enlightened one. The Lord has reigned over the nations; God has sat upon His holy throne. The nobles among the nations have gathered, the people of the God of Abraham. For the protectors of the earth belong to the Lord; He is greatly exalted (Psalm 47).

Commentary: This psalm alludes to the Messianic era, following the war of Gog and Magog. The people of Israel declare that all nations will clap hands and rejoice together with them, for everyone will know that God rules over all the earth. He is above all, everything is under His dominion, and He is awe-inspiring. God will "subdue" the nations by leading them from the ends of the earth to Jerusalem. The land that the Jewish people had formerly possessed will be alloted to them again, and they will return to it. This land is the "pride of Jacob" and the glory [of his descendants], for in it their praiseworthiness shall be revealed to all the nations of the world. "The place that He loves" refers to Jerusalem.

Israel goes on to declare that when they sing God's praises, "the Lord ascends with a blast." In other words, now it will be revealed that God rules over everything that exists. The verse refers to God as "our King" because He had already bound His name to the Jewish people in this world; but on that day He will rule over all the earth.

The term "enlightened one" refers to both Jews and non-Jews; everyone will sing to God. It states previously that all the nations will clap hands, [implying] those who are enlightened and those who are not. [To this objection it could be said that] hand-clapping and raising the voice in joyous song apply to all, whereas the composition of songs and praises is solely the task of the enlightened.

"The Lord has reigned over the nations." Hitherto, God had ruled over Israel alone; now He will rule over all nations. He will "sit on His holy throne" like a sovereign to whom everyone is subordinate. The "nobles" [mentioned in the next verse] are the great individuals of each nation who will be gathered unto the God of Abraham. The Patriarch Abraham is singled out because he was first to make God's name known to the world, as the verse states, "And there Abram called upon the name of God." The term "guardians of the earth" also refers to these great individuals and rulers. [The psalm concludes that] "He is most exalted," for on that day God's absolute supremacy will be established (Rabbi David Kimchi, ad loc.).

A Light unto the Nations

Thus says God, the Lord, He that spread forth the earth and its progeny, Who gives breath to the people upon it and spirit to them who walk therein: I, the Lord, have called upon you in righteousness and will hold your hand and will preserve you and will give you as a covenant-people, as a light unto the nations: to open blind eyes, to release the bound from confinement, and those who sit in darkness from prison (Isaiah 42:5–7).

Commentary: "I will give you as a covenant-people," to sustain all the nations, for in your merit the world endures. The term "covenant" always denotes [a bond that] endures. Similarly, you shall be "a light unto the nations," as it is also written, "Nations shall walk in your light" (Isaiah 60:3). The light is the Torah, which will shine forth to them from Zion. This will sustain the nations in two ways. First, because of [Israel] peace shall be established throughout the world. Thus it is written concerning the Messiah, "He shall declare peace unto the nations" (Zechariah 9:10), and "He will reprove many nations, and they shall beat their swords into ploughshares" (Isaiah 2:4). Second, because through Israel the nations will observe the Seven Commandments of Noah and follow the path of virtue. As the verse states, "Many nations will go and say, 'He will teach us His ways, and we will walk in His paths'" (Isaiah 2:3) (Rabbi David Kimchi, ad loc.).

And He said: It is too small a thing that you should be My servant, to raise up the tribes of Jacob and to restore the beleaguered of Israel; I will also give you as a light unto the nations, to be My deliverance unto the end of the earth (Isaiah 49:6).

Commentary: "I will also give you as a light unto the nations." Your prophecy is destined to be a light unto the nations, for when they see that your words have been fulfilled, they will return to the path of virtue. And it will shine through you to be "My deliverance unto the end of the earth," for with the redemption of Israel, the other nations, too, will be redeemed. This will take place after the war of Gog and Magog, as it is written, "And all flesh shall come to prostrate themselves before Me" (Isaiah 66:23), and "Nations shall walk in your light, and kings in your shining brilliance" (Isaiah 60:3) (Rabbi David Kimchi, ad loc.).

For the Choirmaster, upon the Neginos, a psalm, a song: May the Lord favor us and bless us; may He cause His face to shine unto us, *sela*—to make known Your way throughout the earth, Your salvation among all the nations. The nations will acknowledge the Lord; the nations will acknowledge You, all of them. The world will be glad and sing for joy, because You will judge the nations fairly and govern the people on earth, *sela*. The nations will acknowledge You, O Lord; the nations will acknowledge You, all of them. [Then] the earth will have yielded its produce, [and] the Lord, our God, will bless us. May the Lord bless us, and may all the ends of the earth revere Him (Psalm 67).

Commentary: This psalm views the evolution of mankind to its ultimate goal in three stages. Therefore, it is divided by the interjection *sela* after verses two and five. In the first stage, the Jewish people alone recognizes God and performs His will. The second stage shall be reached when the worship of God has spread among the other nations, and their leaders submit to the supreme authority of God. In the third and final stage, their leaders will abdicate their positions of power entirely, and all humanity will serve God without any intermediary. Then "the earth will have yielded its produce"; mankind will have reached the high spiritual plane at which everyone will render homage to God alone. Thus, [the psalm concludes that] God will bless us, for we will have fulfilled our mission among the nations (Rabbi Samson Raphael Hirsch, *Commentary on the Book of Psalms*, ad loc.).

Essays

4

The Seven Universal Laws of Noah

The narratives, laws, and prophecies contained in the Written Torah are easily accessible (and were once more or less familiar) to both Jews and non-Jews. It is less commonly known that there is an Oral Torah—preserved as the Mishnah, Talmud, Midrash, and the vast literature of Jewish religious law and mysticism—that explains and "fills in the blanks" of the biblical writings. The Seven Universal Laws of Noah are mainly discussed in the Oral Torah.

According to rabbinic tradition, Adam, the first man, possessed all human talents and virtues.[1] His crowning glory was attaining the lofty prophetic state in which God spoke with him directly. Upon being exiled from the Garden of Eden, Adam received the Universal Code directly from God.[2] This code was a lifeline to the state of peace Adam had known in the Garden of

---

1. *Avodah Zarah* 5a; *Bereishis Rabba* 8:10; ibid., 12:5; ibid., 21:1; *Tikkunei Zohar, Tikkun* 57.

2. One of the seven laws, the prohibition of eating a limb from a living animal, actually did not apply to him, since human beings were originally vegetarians. The permission to eat meat was first given after the biblical flood, and this prohibition, too, was given at that time. See Rashi on Genesis 1:29; *Sanhedrin* 59b; *Bereishis Rabba* 24:5; ibid., 34:13 and 18; *Devarim Rabba* 2:25;

Eden, and it was Adam's spiritual legacy to his descendants. By observing its laws, all mankind can enjoy the benefits of a humane society and merit the bliss of the World to Come.[3]

Maimonides relates that the first generation after Adam began to worship the stars and forces of nature, mistakenly thinking that this constituted an even greater tribute to the glory of the Creator. However, their error was not innocent, for in this way they sought to gain various supernatural powers. Eventually, man's awareness of God's Oneness became eclipsed by the preoccupation with angels and astrological forces, until the world completely degenerated to paganism.[4] As a result, the Universal Code was forgotten by most of humanity. However, Noah preserved and upheld the Universal Code. After the great flood, it again served as the basis for human morality.[5] Thus, many ancient moral codes reflect its influence.

The Universal Code was included in the teachings Moses received at Mount Sinai and was passed down from generation to generation by the Sages of Israel until the redaction of the Talmud.[6] Jewish tradition also states that God expressly commanded Moses to teach these seven precepts to the world.[7] Until

---

also note Maimonides, *Mishneh Torah, Melachim* 9:1. However, others contend that Adam received this law as well. See *Sanhedrin* 56b; *Zohar* 1:35b; *Bereishis Rabba* 16:9.

3. *Sanhedrin* 105a; *Tosefta, Sanhedrin* 13:1; *Midrash Tehillim* 9:15; *Mishneh Torah, Teshuvah* 3:5; ibid., *Eidus* 11:10; ibid., *Melachim* 8:11.

4. *Mishneh Torah, Avodas Kochavim* 1:1–2; also note *Sanhedrin* 57a; *Bereishis Rabba* 31:6; Rashi on Genesis 6:11. Concerning sorcery, see *Mishneh Torah, Avodas Kochavim* 11:14–16; *Sefer HaChinuch, Shoftim, Mitzvah* 516, 517; *Derech Hashem* III, 2:8–9.

5. Genesis 6:9. If the people of that generation had been worthy, they would have been given the Torah. See *Shemos Rabba* 30:13; Rabbi Moshe Chaim Luzzatto's *Adir Bamarom* 11b.

6. *Sanhedrin* 56b; *Tosefta Avodah Zarah* 9:4; *Bereishis Rabbah* 16:9; *Devarim Rabbah* 2:17; *Shir HaShirim Rabbah* 1:16. Also see *Mishneh Torah, Melachim* 9:1.

7. *Mishneh Torah, Melachim* 8:10.

the present day, this remains one of the responsibilities of the Jewish people. This responsibility has been neglected primarily due to the adverse circumstances of our exile. Therefore, in these times when many people are searching for spiritual and moral guidance, it is important that these precepts be made known to all. They are:

1. The commandment to establish courts of justice: Originally human nature was devoid of ego and the desire for pleasure as an end in itself.[8] After the first sin, man internalized these tendencies. As a result, in the course of time, interpersonal disputes began to ensue among Adam's descendants.[9] As people strayed further from God, it became increasingly necessary to control man's predilection for violence and immorality. Thus, civilization depends upon the establishment of courts of justice. The proper basis for all societies is the Universal Code, the integrity of which the courts are responsible to uphold.[10]

2. The prohibition against blasphemy: God is infinite and transcendent; His perfection is incomparable to anything in creation. Therefore, God has no need for man's service. The Torah states that the creation of the universe was an act of gratuitous kindness. It follows that disrespect for God does not affect Him in any way.[11] However, such disrespect spiritually undermines both the individual and society as a whole. The supreme human

---

8. Concerning Adam's lofty spiritual level, see *Avodah Zarah* 5a; *Midrash Tehillim* 8:2; ibid., 9:6; *Avos D'Rabbi Nosson* 2:5; *Bereishis Rabba* 21:1; *Bamidbar Rabba* 4:8; *Tikkunei Zohar, Tikkun* 57. However, some sources state that Adam was created with a subtle trace of impurity, in order to possess free will. See *Derech Hashem* I, 3:8.

9. Genesis 4; also note *Derech Hashem* I, 3:8.

10. *Tosefta, Avodah Zara* 9:4; *Mishneh Torah, Melachim* 9:14; Nachmanides on Genesis 34:13; *Sha'alos V'Teshuvos HaRamah, Teshuvah* 10.

11. *Mishneh Torah, Yesodei HaTorah* 1:11; *Sefer HaIkkarim*, chap. 2; *Emunos V'Deos* 1:4; ibid., 2:11; ibid., 3:0; *Derech Hashem* I, 2:1; *Likkutei Moharan* I:52; ibid., I:64.

value is belief in God, which is the root of all virtuous action. When people scorn God, they scorn their own potential for good, as well.[12]

3. The prohibition against idolatry: When God's Oneness is obscured by the deification of nature or any other being or entity, the innate harmony of the universe no longer can be grasped; when God's absolute authority is denied, decisions are governed by self-interest. King David and the kings of Judea used to carry a small Torah scroll with them at all times to show that their sovereignty was only for the sake of serving God, not themselves.[13] This prohibition teaches that civilization cannot be based upon the worship of man, nature, power, pleasure, the state, or any other substitute for God. Societies that do so will be characterized by an abuse of power.

4. The prohibition against murder: The Torah asserts that man is created in the "image of God," and human life is therefore sacred.[14] One who senses the unity of life and its sacredness will be instinctively averse to killing any living being and, certainly, other humans. Thus, the rabbis teach that if one faces the choice between murder or martyrdom, one must choose the latter, for "your blood is not redder than his."[15] When ego—the desire to impose one's will on the world—is left unchecked, it can easily lead to the wanton killing of one's enemies. This is commonplace in most totalitarian regimes. Nevertheless, killing is permitted in self-defense or as legislated by the court to punish those who

---

12. See *Sanhedrin* 56a; *Mishneh Torah, Melachim* 9:3.

13. Deuteronomy 17:18–19; *Sanhedrin* 21b; *Yerushalmi Sanhedrin* 13a; *Tosefta Sanhedrin* 4:4; *Mishneh Torah, Sefer Torah* 7:2; ibid., *Melachim* 3:1.

14. Genesis 1:26–27, 9:5–6; *Sanhedrin* 37a; also note Rabbi Moshe Cordovero's *Tomer Devorah*, chap. 2 and 3, sections of which have been included in the present volume.

15. *Sanhedrin* 74a. However, a Noahide is not obligated to suffer martyrdom for any other commandment, as Maimonides rules in *Mishneh Torah, Melachim* 10:2, according to *Mishneh L'Melech*, ad loc.

violate the Universal Code, for here it serves the greater preservation of human life.[16] Suicide is forbidden because it represents a denial of God's purpose in creating man. Moreover, one's life is not his own property to discard at will; it belongs to God.[17]

5. The prohibition against robbery, theft, and kidnapping: The dignity of each individual is another corollary of the creation of man in God's image. In addition to causing the victim to suffer the loss of his possessions or freedom, the thief or kidnapper deprives the victim of dignity. The proliferation of theft also causes others to lose heart in attempting to better their circumstances through honest labor. The same is true of dishonest business practices. Theft destroys the concept of personal rights, without which the individual cannot feel secure in the world. According to the Torah, it is not enough to regret an act of theft; one must make complete restitution to the victim.[18]

6. The prohibition against sexual immorality: The primary purpose of sexuality is to perpetuate the species, and the basic vehicle for perpetuating the species is the family. Sexual practices that are antithetical to this purpose (such as adultery, incest, homosexuality, and bestiality) are therefore forbidden.[19] But sexuality is not understood by Judaism in utilitarian terms alone. On a mystical level, man and woman represent the principles of giving and receiving. Their union expresses the harmonious combination of opposites.[20] It also symbolizes the

---

16. *Mishneh Torah, Melachim* 9:14.

17. *Baba Kamma* 91b; also see Rashi on Genesis 9:5.

18. *Avodah Zarah* 71b, with Tosefos; however, see Rashi ad loc.; *Mishneh Torah, Melachim* 9:9; *Sefer HaChinuch, Va'eschanan, Mitzvah* 424.

19. *Sanhedrin* 57b–58b; *Tosefta, Avodah Zarah* 9:4; *Mishneh Torah, Melachim* 9:5–7; *Minchas Chinuch* II:209–211; Rashi on Genesis 2:24.

20. *Vayikra Rabba* 29:7; *Sotah* 17a. However, this does not negate the personal factor of love in marriage. Note Genesis 24:67; Ecclesiastes 9:9; *Shir HaShirim Rabbah* 8:6. Most of these sources have been translated to English in Rabbi Aryeh Kaplan's *Made in Heaven: A Jewish Wedding Guide.*

unification of creation and the Creator.[21] Thus, in the ancient
Holy Temple in Jerusalem, the tablets containing the Ten Commandments and the original Torah scroll written by Moses were
contained in a gilded box, over which hovered the male and
female forms of two angels. One of the miracles that took place
in the Holy Temple was that these two angelic forms would
embrace when the actions of the Jewish people were in harmony
with the Divine will.[22]

**7. The prohibition against taking a limb or consuming the
flesh of a living animal:**   Everything in creation plays a role in
the Divine plan. Therefore, one should not disparage any living
being, but rather show mercy to all creatures and try to alleviate
their distress.[23] Slaughtering an animal for food or to otherwise
benefit man is permitted, but not in a cruel manner.[24] According
to Judaism, sensitivity to the suffering of animals is a sign of
spiritual refinement. Both Moses and King David were chosen by
God to lead the Jewish people because as shepherds they had
cared for their flocks with exemplary compassion.[25] The Talmud
tells how a certain Sage was punished by Heaven for speaking
callously to a frightened calf awaiting slaughter.[26] There were
Jewish mystics who wouldn't even kill a mosquito.[27]

21. This is the traditional rabbinic understanding of the Song of Songs. See
Tiferes Yisrael on *Yadayim* 3:5.
22. *Yoma* 4a; *Baba Basra* 99a; *Bamidbar Rabba* 4:13; *Zohar* II, *Terumah*
176a.
23. Rabbi Moshe Cordovero, *Tomer Devorah*, chap. 2; Rabbi Yisrael Baal
Shem Tov, *Tzava'as HaRivash* 12.
24. Cruelty to animals is prohibited by Torah law. See *Shulchan Aruch, Even
HaEzer* 5:14; ibid., *Choshen Mishpat* 272:9 (Ramah); *K'neses HaGedolah* on
Yoreh De'ah 297; *Sefer HaChinuch, Ekev, Mitzvah* 440; ibid., *Ki Seitzei, Mitzvah*
570. Also note *Tomer Devorah*, chap. 3.
25. *Shemos Rabbah* 2:2.
26. *Baba Metziah* 85a.
27. Rabbi Chaim Vital says this of his Kabbalistic mentor, Rabbi Isaac Luria
(the Ari z"l), in *Sha'ar HaMitzvos, Noach* 4b.

In addition to the Seven Universal Laws of Noah, the Jewish tradition considers various spiritual practices to be relevant to all peoples. Although these practices have not been formally codified, they include:

1. Contemplation of God and meditation: Abraham, the first Patriarch, discovered God by contemplating the origin of the universe.[28] Following his example, contemplating nature and searching out its mysteries can be a path to God. Meditating on the omnipresence of the Creator, Who is the source of existence and the only true existence, is another spiritual practice discussed in various Kabbalistic and Chasidic works.[29] However, the ability to attain higher spiritual states depends less upon any particular technique than the degree to which a person has purified himself from worldly desires. For most of us, it is impossible to progress on the inner path without the guidance of a true teacher.

2. Study of Torah: In order to live by the Universal Code, one must study its laws. This outline is really just a starting point. The various ramifications of the Seven Laws are discussed in several other popular works devoted to the subject. The Sages of Israel taught that study of the Torah's laws (including the Universal Code) in a spirit of humility and faith purifies the mind. Therefore, non-Jews who believe in God and strive to live by the Universal Code should study the details of these seven laws, as well as other parts of Torah literature relevant to their spiritual needs and responsibilities.[30]

---

28. *Nedarim* 32a; *Bereishis Rabbah* 39:1; *Zohar* I, 86a.

29. *Kesser Shem Tov* 225; ibid., 273; *Nesiv Mitzvosecha, Nesiv Emunah* 5:1; *Tzava'as HaRivash* 133, 134; *Ohr HaGanuz L'Tzaddikim, B'Ha'aloscha*; ibid., *Vayeira*; ibid., *Mattos*; *Maggid Devarav L'Yaakov* 159; *Ohr HaEmes* 23d. Some of this material has been presented in my anthology of early Chasidic teachings, *The Path of the Baal Shem Tov* (Jason Aronson, 1997).

30. Some authorities consider the study of the laws of Noah to be an offshoot of the prohibition against blasphemy; see Rabbi Menachem Azariah of

3. Prayer: Every person can establish a relationship with God through prayer. One should petition the Creator for all his or her needs, and pray for the welfare of others. Judaism teaches that God receives the prayers of all who sincerely call upon Him. Thus, the Holy Temple in Jerusalem is called "a House of Prayer for all nations."[31] The Chasidic masters taught that through devotional prayer one can come to experience transcendence of self and attachment to God. Rabbi Nachman of Breslov especially recommends going into the forests or fields at night in order to achieve this. (When one cannot leave home, it is beneficial to pray in a quiet, private room where one will not be disturbed.)[32] This practice is associated with Isaac, the second Patriarch, whom the Torah describes as praying alone in the fields.[33]

4. Charity and good deeds: The Talmud considers charity the Divine commandment that equals all the rest.[34] We are all merely custodians of the wealth we possess, the purpose of which is to improve the world as much as possible. In addition to benefiting others, through giving charity and other altruistic acts one overcomes the ego, ceases to be a taker, and becomes a giver. Even without completely pure motives, the one who gives is

---

Pano, *Asarah Maamaros*, p. 66. As for which portions of the Torah non-Jews may or may not study, see *Sanhedrin* 59a, esp. with Meiri, ad loc.; Maharsha on *Shabbos* 31a; *Mishneh Torah, Melachim* 10:9; *Teshuvos Rambam* 364; *Magen Avraham* 334:17; *Teshuvos Rabbi Shmuel Abohav* 75; *Maharatz Chayas, Sotah* 32b; *Teshuvos Rabbi Akiva Eiger* 41; *Teshuvos Machaneh Chaim* 7; also Rabbi Menachem M. Schneerson of Lubavitch, *Likkutei Sichos*, 19 Kislev 5742 (1982); ibid., 19 Kislev 5745 (1984). A section of the latter discourse has been included in the present work.

31. Isaiah 56:7; also note the responsum of Rabbi Moshe Feinstein on whether non-Jews are obligated to pray, *Igros Moshe, Orach Chaim* II:25.

32. See *Likkutei Moharan* I:52; also *Hishtapchus HaNefesh*, Rabbi Nachman's teachings on meditation and prayer. An English translation, *Outpouring of the Soul* (Breslov Research 1980), was authored by Rabbi Aryeh Kaplan.

33. Malbim on Genesis 24:63; *Likkutei Moharan* II:11.

34. *Baba Basra* 9a; *Tosefta, Pe'ah*, chap. 4 (end); *Yerushalmi Pe'ah* 1:2.

meritorious, for the receiver benefits in any case.[35] The rabbis state that not only Israel but people of all nations elicit Divine mercy and protection through their acts of charity and good deeds.[36]

5. Return to God: Judaism teaches that anyone can turn away from evil and come back to God at any moment, no matter what they may have done previously.[37] As the rabbis taught, "Nothing can stand in the way of repentance."[38] The state of spiritual accord that one regains through this act of return is not something artificial. It is the original condition of the soul. King David exemplified repentance, as many of his psalms show. Despair has no true existence, for it denies God's mercy, as well as His ability to alter the laws of nature or to intervene in history.[39] The prophets of Israel taught that God seeks the repentance of Jews and non-Jews alike.[40] In a sense, this is the entire purpose of creation.

6. Joy: According to Judaism, despair is the antithesis of faith. When one truly considers that everything is in God's hands and that everything is for the ultimate good, it is possible to be happy in all circumstances. Thus, the Talmud relates that a certain Sage was known by the name of "This, too" because he

---

35. Rashi on Leviticus 5:17; Baal Shem Tov, as cited in *Turei Zahav, R'ei*.

36. *Baba Basra* 10b; *Tanna D'vei Eliyahu Rabba* 9:1; ibid., 16:1; ibid., 17:19; Rabbi Yehudah HaLevi, *Kuzari* 4:3.

37. Jonah 3:10; *Pesikta* 25; *Yerushalmi Sanhedrin* 11:5; *Mechilta* on Exodus 12:4; *Pirkei Rabbi Eliezer* 10 (24a) with Radal, ad loc.; *Midrash Tanchumah, Vayikra* 8; ibid., *Tzav* 14; *Yalkut Shimoni* II, *Yonah* 1; *Sefer HaTanya, Igeres HaTeshuvah* 2 (91b); also note *Likkutei Moharan* I, 14:5.

38. *Yerushalmi Pe'ah* 1:1; *Yerushalmi Sanhedrin* 10:1; Tosefos on *Baba Metziah* 58b; *Zohar* II, 106a; *Emunos V'De'os* 5:6; *Sichos HaRan* 71.

39. *Likkutei Moharan* II:48.

40. Jonah 4:11; Jeremiah 18:8; *Bamidbar Rabba* 20:1; *Pirkei Rabbi Eliezer* 10 (24a) and 43 (103a) with Radal (10:7); also note *Mishneh Torah, Teshuvah* 1:1, 2:1; *Tomer Devorah*, chap. 4.

would habitually remark, "This, too, is for the good" (*Taanis* 21a, concerning Nachum Ish Gamzu). The prophets of Israel declared that all of history is leading to a time when evil, suffering, and strife will cease. Then, all the good that mankind has accomplished will be gathered together, and Godliness will be revealed to all. This is the Messianic era. When a person realizes that by following God's precepts he is helping to bring the world to this state of perfection, he should be especially joyous.

There is a Chasidic story that illustrates this point. Once there was a poor Jew who was known for his great joy. Although constantly in debt and beset with difficulties, he always managed to remain happy. Some of his neighbors, who were having a hard time themselves, found this a bit annoying.

"You're the poorest man in town," they remarked. "Why are you so full of joy?"

"I borrowed it," he admitted, "from the better days ahead!"[41]

May we soon see the days of true joy, when at last there will be peace between nations, and "the knowledge of God fills the earth like the water that covers the sea" (Isaiah 11:9).

---

41. Based on *Sefer Oneg Shabbos* (Rabbi Ephraim of Pshedbarz), *Hosafos*, p. 525, regarding Rabbi Aharon of Kiblitch. Also note *Parparaos L'Chochmah* on *Likkutei Moharan* I:24, *he'arah* 15.

5

The Merciful One Desires the Heart

A final note about the Universal Code: why is the religion offered to the nations of the world couched in the form of seven laws, six of which are prohibitions? Couldn't these ideals have been formulated in a more positive, general way? The same question can be applied to the entire Torah, which consists of 613 scriptural commandments and countless rabbinic decrees set forth in the Talmud. Most of these laws are prohibitions. Why does Judaism put so much emphasis on restrictive law?

At the most basic level, the Torah is more concerned with preventing harm than with maximizing individual freedom of action. Although every person is unique, possessing value and dignity, this uniqueness is inextricably part of a greater context. As civilized human beings, we are responsible not only unto ourselves, but also to those with whom we share the world and its resources. Ecology has demonstrated the error of ignoring our environment. A similar concern applies to the moral sphere.

Everyone seeks personal fulfillment; however, it is necessary to do so in a way that avoids harm to others and ultimately contributes to the common good. Given the innate selfishness of man's lower nature, virtually all social groups have formulated laws to protect us from ourselves. Inevitably, most of those laws are restrictive. It is easier to fool ourselves when given a noble-sounding principle than when given a specific law by which to act. In the twilight of moral ambiguity, when a person falls down, someone else usually gets hurt, too.

The Mishna says, "Pray for the welfare of the government, for if not for the fear of it, people would eat each other alive" (*Avos* 3:2). No society can function without laws, and both the Torah and the Universal Code are plans for an ideal society. However, the Torah and the Universal Code are not the same as other legal systems. Having been given by Divine revelation, they accurately reflect the needs of humanity. Moreover, the precepts of the Torah and the Universal Code enable us to establish a unique bond with God. By performing the Divine will, we actually become one with God at the level of action.[1]

However, action is only one dimension of existence. What about the mind and heart? How does a religion of laws address these aspects of human nature? In fact, God does not want us to serve Him only by conforming to behaviors that can be regulated by law. "The Merciful One desires the heart," taught the rabbis of the Talmud.[2] Even the Mishna (the basis of rabbinic law) includes a section that deals with self-improvement and nonlegalistic aspects of Divine service: *Pirkei Avos* (*Chapters of the Fathers*). The depths of the heart cannot be touched by a master-slave relationship. A Chasid (pious individual) is, by definition, one who does more than the law requires.[3] To establish an intimate relationship with God, we must not only fulfill His explicit will, but also "seek His face" (Psalms 105:4).

It is interesting that the Torah uses the same term—Chasid—for the non-Jew who follows the Seven Universal Laws of Noah.

---

1. *Kuzari* I:79, 98, 115; Rabbi Yisrael Baal Shem Tov, *Ner Mitzvah* 13a; *Kesser Shem Tov* 111; *Likkutei Halachos, Netilas Yadaim Shel Shacharis* 4:11; ibid., *Nefilas Apayim* 4:9, et al.

2. *Sanhedrin* 106b; also note Nachmanides on *Vayikra* 19:2.

3. *Niddah* 17a, *Tosefos*, ad loc.; also note *Be'er Heitev* on *Shulchan Aruch, Orach Chaim* 260:2; *Likkutei Dibburim* I:68a.

The truth is that these laws are obligatory for all; however, not only are most people ignorant of this, they prefer to remain that way. An individual who searches for God and chooses to adhere to these precepts is going out of his way, leaving aside the false beliefs and negative influences of his environment. Moreover, the term "Chasid" also suggests that even for the non-Jew there is a dimension of Divine service that must be volitional, and, as such, not regulated by law. God leaves it up to the individual to approach Him through prayer and meditation, charity, and good deeds.

On a deeper level, our relationship with God through the exercise of free will refines and transforms creation.[4] The world in its present state is a confusion of good and evil, truth and falsehood. Human nature is torn between opposite poles. We possess an inclination for relationship and harmony and a contrary inclination for strife and selfish craving. The former could be thought of as "positive energy," in that it seeks unity, and the latter as "negative energy," in that it seeks separateness and disunity. However, these same polarities may reverse themselves. The "positive energy" can turn into a tendency to abdicate personal responsibility through identification with charismatic false leaders, mass movements, etc. The "negative energy" can turn into a more individualistic tendency to develop our creativity or to take a stand on a matter of principle. In any case, our spiritual starting point is usually a state of existential conflict.

Torah law separates the permissible from the forbidden, the pure from the impure, tempers human passions, and establishes civilization. Through devotion to the fulfillment of the Divine will, we clarify and distill the conflicting tendencies of human nature. In Jewish mysticism, this process is called *taharah*—

---

4. *Zohar* I, 4a, I:61a, II:32b, II:58a, II:65b; *Tikkunei Zohar, Tikkun* 70 (131a); *Toldos Yaakov Yosef, Vayeira* (17a); *Likkutei Halachos, Sukkah v'Lulav* 6:11.

purification.[5] This spiritual work makes the individual a vessel for higher consciousness, and the world a dwelling place for the Divine Presence.[6]

Judaism asserts that the main point of living in this world is to use our freedom of choice in the proper manner. "I have set before you this day a blessing and a curse, life and death: choose life!" (Deuteronomy 30:19). Free choice requires the presence of evil. "Turn from evil and do good," the Psalmist declares (Psalms 34:15). However, evil ultimately plays a positive role, for the antithesis of good is the necessary vehicle for choosing the good. When this process of refinement is complete, evil itself will be transformed.[7]

Light cannot be recognized without darkness, and good cannot be recognized without evil.[8] The verse states, "Then I saw that wisdom excels folly as light excels darkness" (Ecclesiastes 2:13). This also may be rendered, "Then I saw that the superiority of wisdom that comes from folly is like the superiority of light that emerges from darkness." It is obvious that wisdom is superior to folly. The point here is that wisdom must emerge from folly, and that, in fact, this sort of wisdom is superior to that which is gained without struggle. Just as in the Jewish tradition night precedes day, so one cannot come to the positive without passing through the negative. Thus, it may be said that the negative gives birth to the positive.[9]

---

5. *Likkutei Moharan* I:51.

6. This principle pervades Kabbalistic thought, especially pietistic works such as *Reishis Chochmah, Sha'arei Kedushah, Sefer HaBris*, etc. In Chasidic literature, see *Likkutei Moharan* I:21 (sec. 2) and I:49 (sec. 4); Rabbi Shneur Zalman of Liadi, *Sefer HaTanya*, chap. 36, and *Likkutei Torah, Shir HaShirim* 41a; Rabbi Dov Ber of Lubavitch, *Shaarei Teshuvah* II:62c, and *Toras Chaim, Shemos*, p. 335b; et al.

7. *Zohar* I, 4a; *Pardes Rimmonim* 31:5; *Degel Machaneh Ephraim, Tzav; Likkutei Moharan* I, 22:11; *Likkutei Halachos, Mincha* 7:32.

8. *Shabbos* 77b; *Zohar* I, *Bereishis* 22b, 32a; *Zohar* II, 184a, 187a; *Zohar* III, 80b; *Tikkunei Zohar, Tikkun* 70. *Likkutei Halachos, Nefilas Apayim* 4:21.

9. Rabbi Moshe Chaim Luzzatto, *Daas Tevunos* 166a, 185a; *Adir Bamarom*

Actually, this is a transformative process. To draw upon yet another analogy, the dualism of exile and redemption clearly demonstrates this principle. The children of Israel, through their experience of slavery in Egypt, came to appreciate freedom. Suffering removed their dross, their attachment to physicality, until their true spiritual nature could be revealed. Having undergone this process of purification, the children of Israel were a fit vessel to receive the Torah, which represents the opposite of slavery. The Sages equate the Torah with freedom, for it liberates the Jew from enslavement to the ego and physicality, and enables him or her to establish a relationship with God.[10] In his profound study of the Book of Exodus as a mystical paradigm, the Maharal of Prague describes exile as "the womb of redemption."[11] It is interesting that he does not compare exile to the husk that surrounds the fruit, the "bad" that surrounds the "good," etc.; rather, he compares it to the womb. Perhaps this is because, paradoxically, the redemption transcended the very dualism of exile and redemption. Not only did the positive element emerge from its antithesis, but an entirely new reality came into being. This is the concept of "giving birth."

Thus, the Maharal's statement has several implications. Seventy members of the Patriarch Jacob's family had descended to Egypt—the most morally corrupt, albeit intellectually advanced, society in the world.[12] The "pure" entered the realm of the "impure." However, the children of Israel who stood at Mount Sinai were different than their ancestors in many ways. The

---

II:38–39; *Igros Pischei Chochmah V'Daas*, p. 336; *K'lach Pischei Chochmah* IV:3; *Likkutei Moharan* I, 38:4, 49:1; *Likkutei Halachos, Mincha* 7:22; ibid., *Milah* 3; Rabbi Tzadok HaKohen, *Resisei Lailah* 13, 17, 24, 45; *Tzidkas HaTzaddik* 4, 11, 27, 76.

10. *Avos* 6:2, citing Exodus 32:16: "'The script was the script of God engraved [*charus*] on the Tablets.' Do not read *charus* [engraved] but *chairus* [freedom], for no man is freer than he who engages in the study of Torah."

11. *Gevuros Hashem*, chap. 4 and 5.

12. Genesis 46:27; Exodus 1:5; also note *Sifra, Acharei* 9.

"impure" had re-entered the realm of the "pure"—with a certain advantage. Spiritually, they had been refined through suffering. Numerically, their population had increased to more than three million men, women, and children. Politically, although twelve tribes had entered Egypt, one nation emerged. The redemption had not merely restored a value that had been lacking. Something new had been gained.

The same dynamic of the negative giving birth to the positive applies to the moral sphere. Only through the possibility of moral failure can one come to appreciate the good—and in so doing transcend moral dualism and enter into the realm of Oneness that is pure good.[13] The state of reality in which the good must be distilled from the bad through the exercise of free will is but an intermediate stage. Ultimately, discord will give birth to harmony. When this takes place, the inner aspect of Torah that underlies its legalistic dimension will also become fully revealed.[14] This is what Isaiah alluded to as the "new teaching" that God will reveal during the Messianic era, and that the Kabbalists termed *Torah D'Atika Stimah*, the Torah of the Hidden Ancient One (Isaiah 51:4).[15] It is the dimension of Torah through which the ultimate reality will be apprehended by all.

---

13. *Likkutei Moharan* I:51.

14. Rabbi Shneur Zalman of Liadi, *Torah Ohr, Shemos* 49a; *Likkutei Eitzos, Inyan Torah* 18.

15. However, this does not mean that the laws of the Torah will be suspended. See *Mishneh Torah, Yesodei HaTorah* 11:3; *Sanhedrin* 90a; *Tosefta, Sanhedrin* 14:4; *Emunos V'De'os* 3:8 (end). According to the Midrash, it indicates a temporary innovation in a particular law (*Vayikra Rabba* 13:3, with *Anaf Yosef* and *Chiddushei Radal*). Others understand it as a reference to the teachings that the Messiah will proclaim to the nations (Abarbanel, Metzudas David, ad loc.). *Torah D'Atika S'timah* indicates the most profound, hidden dimension of Divine truth. See *Pesachim* 119a; Maharal, *Tiferes Yisrael*, chap. 7; *Maggid Devarav L'Yaakov* 6; *Zohar* II, *Sifra D'Tzniusah*, chap. 4, 178a, discussed in *Likkutei Moharan* I:21 (sec. 10), I:49 (sec. 6); *Chayei Moharan* 289. Our interpretation is based on Rabbi Gedaliah Kenig's *Chayei Nefesh*, chap. 29. In a similar vein, note Rabbi Tzadok HaKohen, *Pri Tzaddik, Parah* 6.

Every Friday night most Jewish congregations recite the Kabbalistic song, "Come, my Beloved, let us greet the Bride." One stanza of this deeply mystical composition refers to the Sabbath as "last in deed, first in thought."[16] The Sabbath is a foretaste of the World to Come, a time when the ultimate purpose of creation begins to shine into our hearts.[17] All conflict is stilled, peace reigns, and the unity of all things within God is revealed. This Divine Oneness is both the source and essential nature of all creation, and its realization is life's highest goal.[18]

16. Rabbi Shlomo Alkabetz, "*L'cha Dodi,*" based on *Sefer Yetzirah* 1:7.

17. *Berachos* 57b; *Kesser Shem Tov* 401.

18. *Likkutei Moharan* I:58, I:64, II:2, II:83; *Likkutei Halachos, Mincha* 4; ibid., *Shabbos* 7:43; ibid., *Kalei HaKerem* 2:3; *Daas Tevunos*, pp. 28–29.

6

Tefillin: Paradigm of Unity

The Torah requires Jewish males above the age of thirteen to put on tefillin every day, except on the Sabbath and Jewish holidays. (Tefillin are a pair of black leather boxes, one of which is strapped to the left arm and the other worn above the forehead.) The scriptural passages these boxes contain declare the fundamental Jewish beliefs in God's Oneness, the uniqueness of Israel, and the obligation to love and revere the Creator. The commandment to wear tefillin is restricted to the Jewish people. What could be more particularist?

Nevertheless, tefillin also have a connection to non-Jews. There is a verse that states, "And all the nations of the Earth shall see that the name of God is called upon you, and they shall fear you" (Deuteronomy 28:10). The Talmud comments that this refers to the tefillin of the head (which are visible to all) (*Berachos* 6a according to Rashi). A person encountering this teaching for the first time would probably ask several questions: Why is it important for other nations to see that God's name is called upon Israel? Why should Israel's relationship to God be a matter of concern to anyone else? Why should the recognition of Israel by the nations be evoked through the precept of tefillin? Moreover, why should this be an occasion for fear? Certainly there is no threat posed by these ritual objects.

Perhaps the Talmud's view of the effect of tefillin upon the non-Jewish nations may be understood better in the light of another rabbinic teaching: "The Holy One, blessed be He, only sent the Jewish people into exile so that through them the nations of the world would also receive blessing" (*Zohar* I, *Vayechi* 244a). By observing the tefillin—symbols of Israel's dedication to God—all nations may come to revere Him. As a consequence of this reverence, they, too, will heed the commandments incumbent upon them. When civilization is established according to the Divine will, the possibility of world peace will no longer seem remote. Thus, when understood in this broader context, the tefillin, a paradigm of Jewish particularism, are inextricably bound up with a greater universalism.

Rabbi Samson Raphael Hirsch, one of the most original Jewish thinkers of the 19th century and a profound humanist, also felt that this scriptural verse implied the responsibility of Israel as a "light unto the nations." In his *Commentary on the Torah*, he states:

> God's wish is to mark you for himself; that is, for His purposes on behalf of mankind. He wishes to have you be a holy nation, a nation belonging to Him; a nation that keeps away from all things base and vulgar; a nation doing only what is good; a model nation—so that all the other nations may see that the name of God has been called upon you. Let all the nations of the world see what it means to be "the people of God"; what it means if an entire nation—all its members, great and small—subordinates its existence and aspirations, both as individuals and as a collectivity, entirely to the will of God. Let them see the blessings and the power that will come to such a nation—a "tefillin-bearing nation," as the Sages put it (*Menachos* 35b).

Fear of God as a religious value has received a lot of bad press in recent times. We usually think of fear as the prized commodity of tyrants (whether they rule over nations, classrooms, or dining tables). However, in traditional Jewish thought, fear of God has an entirely different value. The Creator's intent toward his creatures is purely beneficent, as the Psalmist declares, "God is good to all, and His mercy is upon all that He has made" (Psalms 145:9). Love of God arises from the perception of God's immanence, His nearness and favor. Fear of God entails awe of the Infinite One to Whom every created thing is incomparable, and submission to the Divine Will that transcends mortal understanding. Because God is always beyond us, fear is the higher perception.[1] Moreover, at the level of action, it is fear of God that can enable the person ensnared in a moral dilemma to abdicate self-serving desires and choose what he or she believes to be the objective good. By their example, the Jewish people are supposed to teach reverence for God to the rest of the world. This purpose, the Talmud suggests, is related to the wearing of tefillin.

There is a deeper reason why it is important for all nations of the world to relate to this distinctively Jewish precept. The tefillin uniquely express the mystery of God's Oneness, which, by definition, encompasses all that exists. The main scriptural text the tefillin contain is the declaration: "Hear, O Israel, the Lord, our God, the Lord is One" (Deuteronomy 6:4). The *Zohar* (one of the classic works of Jewish mysticism) describes the revelation of Divine Oneness in terms of a *Yichudah Ila'ah* (Higher Unification) and a *Yichudah Tata'ah* (Lower Unification). What is the difference between these two levels? Chasidic works explain that the Higher Unification is effected when all plurality is subsumed within God's Oneness. The Lower Unification is effected when God's Oneness is revealed to be the root and essence of every particular thing. By way of example, the former teaches us that all drops of water are part of the sea; the latter, that the "essence" of the sea is contained in each drop.[2]

---

1. See *Likkutei Moharan* I:185; ibid., II:6, regarding the aspects of *Ayeh* and *Malei*.

2. Based on *Maggid Devarav L'Yaakov* 66; *Kesser Shem Tov* 65; *Likkutim Yekarim* 161; also see *Shaar HaYichud V'HaEmunah* in *Sefer HaTanya*.

Master Kabbalist Rabbi Moshe Cordovero elucidates this concept in his *Ohr Ne'erav* (Part 6:1):

> When the Creator is called One, it is in this sense: the Creator is present in actuality within all things, while all things are present within Him in potential. He is the beginning and cause of all existence. Thus, the Creator possesses unity without change by addition or subtraction, similar to the number one. Just as the number one is necessary for all numbers, for no number could exist without it, so is the Creator the imperative existence. If the number one should be eliminated, all numbers would be eliminated; whereas if [all subsequent] numbers should be eliminated, the one would not be eliminated. This is the power of unity. [However, the analogy is imperfect, for] God is not a number. . . . Should creation be eliminated, God would still exist, since He has no need of creation and His existence is sufficient unto itself.

It follows that the revelation of God's Oneness cannot be complete until all existence comes to recognize the Creator, Who is the essential reality and the ultimate existence.

This aspiration is expressed by a Kabbalistic prayer that many Chasidim recite before putting on tefillin. Although its author is unknown, it may be found in *Siddur Tefillah Yesharah*, the prayerbook edited by the early Chasidic master Rabbi Aharon of Zelichov. It is also included in the *Siddur Chemdas Yisrael*, edited by Rabbi Chaim Elazar Shapira of Munkatch. The term "Lower Divine Presence" alludes to the concept of the Lower Unification, corresponding to God's imminence. The term "Upper Divine Presence" alludes to the concept of the Upper Unification, corresponding to God's transcendence. The anonymous author relates these two perceptions to the tefillin of the hand and those of the head. The prayer states:

> Thus do I put on the tefillin of the hand in order to bring all the nations under the dominion of the Lower Divine Presence (*Shechina Tata'ah*), and the tefillin of the head to bring all the

nations under the dominion of the Upper Divine Presence (*Shechina Ila'ah*). As it is written, "For You, God, are above all the earth; You absolutely transcend all other powers" (Psalms 97:9).

Another universalist aspect of tefillin is suggested by the Talmud's specific mention of the tefillin of the head. According to a legal tradition attributed to Moses himself, this leather box is inscribed with the Hebrew letter *shin* on each side. One *shin* has the standard three branches, while the other has four. This four-branched *shin* has no other place in Jewish ritual or practice. Together, the branches of these two *shins* are seven in number. Significantly, this corresponds to many other sevens in Judaism: the seven branches of the Menorah (candalabrum) in the Holy Temple, the seven days of creation, the seven colors of the rainbow—and the Seven Laws of Noah. I would like to suggest that this allusion to the Universal Code is the message that non-Jews are meant to receive by observing the tefillin worn by the nation of Israel. Through their observance of these laws, the entire world, which was created in seven days, will be permeated with the light of God's Oneness.[3]

The symbolism of the tefillin thus points to the key elements of our basic thesis. Through the medium of the Jewish people, all of humanity will come to serve God by living according to the Seven Laws of Noah. At last peace will be established among the nations, and mankind will be able to devote its energies entirely to positive endeavors. This is the Messianic era, of which the Prophet Isaiah said, "The knowledge of God shall fill the earth, like the water that covers the sea" (Isaiah 11:9). Thus, every person will ultimately experience the mystical unifications to which the tefillin allude, each according to his or her deeds and spiritual level.[4]

---

3. This is implied by *Likkutei Moharan* I:21.
4. *Likkutei Moharan* I:21 (end) and I:27.

7

Prayers

INTRODUCTION

One of the central themes of Rosh Hashanah (the Jewish New Year) is the recognition of God as Supreme King over the Jewish people and all creation. This concept is reflected in the first three prayers presented here. During the Talmudic period (approximately two thousand years ago), they were part of the Rosh Hashanah prayer service. In medieval times, it became customary to conclude each daily service with the third prayer, best known as "*Aleinu.*" Today, this custom is observed by virtually the entire Jewish people. According to many rabbinic authorities, including Rav Hai Gaon (939–1038), the "*Aleinu*" prayer was composed by Joshua after he led the Israelites across the Jordan River into the Holy Land. Thus, its universal message is intimately bound up with the ingathering of the Jewish people to the land of Israel.[1] The condition of world peace that this prayer anticipates will be realized during the Messianic era.

---

1. See *Otzar HaTefillos, Aleinu Shel Shacharis, Iyun Tefillah* citing *Kol Bo* and *Teshuvas HaGaonim; Likkutei Halachos, Orach Chaim, Devarim HaNohagim BiSe'udah* 4:5.

The other prayers we have selected were authored by Rabbi
Nosson Sternhartz of Nemirov (1780–1844), foremost disciple
of the reknowned Chasidic master Rabbi Nachman of Breslov
(1772–1810). They are part of his *Likkutei Tefillos*, a collection of
profound and inspiring prayers based upon Rabbi Nachman's
discourses. *Likkutei Tefillos* is presently being translated into
English as *The Fiftieth Gate* by Avraham Greenbaum, and I have
also translated a selection of Rabbi Nosson's prayers on various
themes in a work entitled *The Flame of the Heart*. Both are
published by the Breslov Research Institute of Jerusalem.

Rosh Hashanah plays a central role in Rabbi Nachman's
teachings. In fact, he once remarked, "My entire mission is Rosh
Hashanah" (*Chayei Moharan* 403–406). This statement may be
understood in many ways. Perhaps, on the most basic level,
Rabbi Nachman meant that just as Rosh Hashanah represents a
new beginning in the reckoning of years, so could his teachings
enable the seeker to make a new start in life, regardless of his or
her past. Another implication is that, since the first man and
woman were created on Rosh Hashanah, Rabbi Nachman's
teachings address all of humanity. Therefore, it is not surprising
that the universalism found in the Rosh Hashanah prayers is
reflected in his works, as well as those of his disciples.

SOURCES

Rosh Hashanah Prayers

O God and God of our fathers: may You reign over the entire universe in Your glory, and be exalted over all the earth in Your splendor. Reveal Yourself in the majesty of Your power to all the inhabitants of Your terrestrial world. May everything created know that You created it; may everything formed know that You formed it; and may every being that possesses the breath of life in its nostrils declare, "The Lord, God of Israel, is King, and His kingship extends over all" (*Musaf* service, *Rosh Hashanah*).

Then they shall all come to serve You, and they shall bless Your glorious name. They shall speak of Your righteousness in the faraway islands, and nations that knew You not shall seek You. All ends of the earth will praise You and forever say, "May God be exalted." They will abandon their idols and be ashamed of their statues and turn to serve You with a common accord.

Those who seek Your face will revere You as long as the sun exists; they will recognize the power of Your sovereignty and teach understanding to those who have gone astray. They will speak of Your might, and they will extol You, Who transcends all rulers. In Your presence they will pray with awe, and they will crown You with a crown of splendor. The mountains will burst forth with song, and the distant islands will shout for joy that You are King. They will accept the yoke of Your kingship upon themselves, and exalt You among the assembled people. Those who are far will hear and draw close, and they will present You with a crown of royalty (ibid.).

Therefore, we hope unto You, Lord our God, to speedily behold the splendor of Your might: may false gods be removed from the earth, so that idolatry will be utterly cut off; may the world attain perfection (*tikkun*) through the kingship of the Almighty, so that all humanity will call upon Your name, and all the wicked of the earth will turn to You. All the world's inhabitants will recognize and know that unto You every knee shall bend, every tongue shall swear (Isaiah 45:23). Before You, O Lord our God, they will bow and prostrate themselves; they will render homage to the glory of Your name, and they will all accept upon themselves the yoke of Your kingship, that You shall reign over them—soon and forever. For dominion is Yours, and forever You shall reign in glory, as it is written in Your Torah: God shall reign for all eternity (Exodus 15:18). And it is said: God will be King over all the world—on that day, God will be One, and His name will be One (Zechariah 14:9) (ibid.).

RABBI NOSSON'S PRAYERS

Peaceful Dialogue

Our God and God of our fathers, Master of Peace, King unto Whom peace belongs—may it be Your will to bestow peace upon Your people, Israel. Let peace abound and spread through all the world until there is no longer any hatred, jealousy, conflict, strife, or hostility between one person and another. May there be only great love and peace among all people. May we all recognize the love that others bear for us and know that they seek our good and our love and truly desire our lasting success.

Then we will be able to get together, each person with his friend, to engage in genuine dialogue and explain the truth to each other. We will arouse one another to contemplate man's lot in this world very carefully. For this world passes by as quickly as the blink of an eye, like a passing shadow—and not the shadow of a tree or a wall, but the shadow of a flying bird. Let every person and his friend discuss the ultimate futility of worldly desires and vanities, and realize the true purpose of the soul's descent to this lowly world. Let us speak at length with each other in a spirit of love, brotherhood, and deep affection, truthfully, from the depths of our hearts, without any desire to win arguments or to provoke each other at all.

Through such dialogue may we all return to You sincerely, throwing away our "idols of silver and gold." May we cease to follow the crookedness of our hearts for evil and no longer waste our lives in the pursuit of wealth; neither may we chase after luxuries, nor try to amass riches. Then the spirit of folly will be banished from our hearts, and peace will grow and spread throughout the world. All Israel will return to You in complete repentance, according to Your beneficent will. All the nations of the world, too, will be spiritually awakened, and they will recognize the ultimate truth. They will all return to You and accept the yoke of Your kingship upon themselves. Thus, the prophecy will be fulfilled, "For I will convert the nations to a pure speech, that they shall all call upon the name of God and serve Him with a common accord" (*Likkutei Tefillos* I:27).

Unity in Diversity

Master of Peace, King unto Whom peace belongs, Who "makes peace and creates everything" (Isaiah 45:7), help us always to grasp the Divine attribute of peace. May there be perfect peace between every person and his fellow, between every man and wife, without any trace of strife, even in the hidden depths of the heart, among all of humanity. For You make peace at the loftiest levels, binding together opposite forces such as fire and water in perfect unity, and in Your wondrous ways, You make peace between them. Thus may You draw great peace upon us and upon everyone in the world, until all opposing views unite in great peace and love. May they become incorporated into one encompassing perception and one heart, in order to bring us closer to You and Your Torah in truth, and may we all "form one band in order to perform Your will wholeheartedly." God, [one of Whose holy names is] "Peace," bless us with peace, and in this way confer upon us all blessings and beneficial influences and bring about our complete deliverance (ibid., I:95).

The Hidden Tzaddikim

Merciful God, make us worthy of having the hidden Torah and the hidden *tzaddikim*[2] revealed to us. Even if the world does not

---

2. "The righteous." In this context, the term refers to the great spiritual teachers who not only have perfected themselves, but are capable of elevating

yet deserve to glimpse this hidden light, nevertheless, deal with us mercifully and not according to the dictates of strict justice. Awaken Your true mercy and kindness on our behalf, and, in Your goodness and graciousness, help us to become worthy of the revelation of the hidden *tzaddikim* and the hidden Torah. For You know, O God, that we have no hope and nothing upon which to rely in these times except the hidden *tzaddikim* and the hidden Torah. Only they can protect us now, in the depths of this bitter exile, in the darkness that precedes the advent of the Messiah. Pity us in Your mercy, arouse Your compassion for us, and help us to overcome the evil in our hearts completely, according to Your beneficent will. May our deeds find favor in Your eyes, so that even in this world we may experience the light that is hidden and stored away for the *tzaddikim*. As it is written, "Light is sown for the righteous, and joy for the straight of heart" (Psalms 97:11) and, "Say of the righteous that it shall be well, for they will eat the fruit of what they have brought about" (Isaiah 3:10).

Send peace to Israel; remove all strife from the world, until there is such peace that those who are far will be drawn near, in order to serve and revere You. Even those who are most distant from holiness, who are sunken and befouled in all sorts of abominations, in mud and in filth—may they all be spiritually awakened. From the very place in which they find themselves, may they return to You through the power of the true *tzaddikim*, who continually strive to reveal Your Godliness and Your dominion to all humanity, and who make peace between Israel and their Father in Heaven.

Even now, in this world, draw forth the wondrous peace that You shall reveal in the Ultimate Future, as the prophet states, "And the wolf will dwell with the lamb, and the leopard will lie down with the kid, and the bull and the lion and the fatling together, and a small child shall lead them. They will do no harm,

---

others from their confusions and inner obstacles, ultimately enabling them to perceive Godliness.

and they will not destroy in all My holy mountain; for the earth will be full of the knowledge of God as the waters cover the sea" (Isaiah 11:6–9). And the verse shall be fulfilled, "Peace, peace unto the one who is distant and the one who is near, says God, and I will heal him" (Isaiah 57:19). "Great peace is granted to those who love Your Torah, and there is no stumbling block for them (Psalms 119:165). God will give strength to His people; God will bless His people with peace" (Psalms 29:11). Amen, *sela* (ibid., I:33).

The Universal Sabbath

May we receive the Sabbath in a spirit of holiness, with joy and gladness and a whole heart. Show us Your favor, O God, and allow no worry or sorrow to disturb our day of rest. May we greatly rejoice on each Sabbath with true joy, with happiness and song, gladness and delight. Help us to draw forth the holiness of the Sabbath into the days of the week, so that we may be joyous even then, delighting and rejoicing in You at all times. Then God's simple Oneness will be revealed to the world, so that everyone may know and believe that all diversity comes from the One, may He be blessed and exalted forever. "And every created thing will know that You created it, and every formed thing will know that You formed it. And every being that has the breath of life in its nostrils will declare, 'The Lord, God of Israel, is King, and His kingship extends over all.'"

May God's Oneness be revealed to all through Your people, Israel, whom You have chosen as One Nation from all the nations on the face of the earth. For "You are One, and Your name is One; and who is like unto Your people, Israel, one nation in the world?" Just as Your Oneness is revealed in this world below through Your holy people, Israel, may Your Oneness be revealed above in all the spiritual worlds. May You remove all conflict and strife forever and bring us peace (ibid., II:2).

Afterword

It seems fitting to conclude this work with a well-known teaching of Hillel, one of the Sages of the Mishna. He states: "If I am not for myself, who will be for me?" In the context of our discussion, this asserts the primacy of Jewish particularism. Both as individuals and as a nation, we must retain our identity and purpose. The basis for this is the Torah, without which the Jews are bereft of any enduring message or distinctiveness. History has too often shown that every Jewish movement that abandoned the Torah eventually ceased to be Jewish at all. However, Hillel continues, "If I am only for myself, what am I?" While seeking to ensure our own physical and spiritual survival, we must at the same time extend our compassion to all humanity, indeed, to all living beings. It is not enough for this sentiment, however noble, to be enshrined in our hearts; it must bear results. Therefore, Hillel's teaching concludes with a call to action: "And if not now, when?" (*Mishna: Avos* 1:14).

Biographies

Alter, R. Yehudah Aryeh Leib (1847–1905): One of the most distinguished leaders of the Polish Chasidic dynasty of Ger, R. Yehudah Aryeh Leib was raised by his grandfather Rabbi Yitzhak Meir Alter of Ger after his father's untimely death. His Talmudic commentaries and Chasidic discourses, both entitled *S'fas Emes* (*The Lip of Truth*), are considered modern classics. R. Yehudah Aryeh Leib was succeeded by his son, R. Avraham Mordechai, fourth Gerer Rebbe and author of a collection of Chasidic discourses entitled *Imrei Emes* (*Words of Truth*).

Azkari, R. Elazar (1533–1600): Born in Constantinople to a family of Portugese refugees, R. Elazar Azkari emigrated to Safed, Israel, where he wrote the classic of Jewish ethics, *Sefer Chareidim*. A Kabbalist and ascetic, Rabbi Elazar composed numerous religious poems, the most famous of which is *Yedid Nefesh*. He also authored several talmudic commentaries and a commentary to *Lamentations* that are longer extant.

Azulai, R. Chaim David Yosef (1724–1806): Best known by his Hebrew acronym, the Chida was born and raised in Jerusalem, where he became the youngest member of Beth El, a Kabbalistic brotherhood led by the saintly Rabbi Shalom Sharabi (approx. 1700–1777). Author of numerous works, he is most famous for his *Shem HaGedolim*, a comprehensive bibliography of Torah works; glosses to the *Shulchan Aruch* in *Birkei Yosef* and *Machazik Beracha; Nachal Eshkol* on the Five Megillos; and *Pesach Einayim* on the Talmud. An emissary on behalf of the communities of Hebron and Jerusalem, the Chida often traveled to Livorno (Leghorn), where he spent the last six years of his life.

Baal Shem Tov (R. Yisrael Ben Eliezer) (1698–1760): Founder of the Chasidic movement, R. Yisrael was probably the most influential Jewish mystic since the Ari (R. Yitzchak Luria). Aside from his reputation as a wonder-worker and healer, he was a profound thinker who revolutionized Jewish life by guiding those seeking the loftiest heights of spirituality, while also reaching out to the lost and disenfranchised. His key disciples included R. Dov Ber (Maggid of Mezeritch), R. Yaakov Yosef of Polonoye, R. Pinchas of Koretz, and his two illustrious grandsons, R. Baruch of Medzhibuzh and R. Moshe Chaim Ephraim of Sudylkov. They preserved many of the Baal Shem Tov's teachings. *Kesser Shem Tov* by R. Aharon of Zelichov was an early attempt to gather these teachings together in one volume.

Bachaye, Rabbeinu (or Bachya) (1263–1340): R. Bachaye Ben Asher was a *dayan* (rabbinical judge) in Saragossa. A student of the Rashba, he is best known for his *Commentary on the Torah*, first published in Naples in 1492. His writings reflect a strong Kabbalistic orientation.

Baraisa (Aramaic: "Outside"): A teaching of the Sages not included in the Mishna. Several collections of *baraisos* are the *Mechilta of R. Yishmael* and the *Mechilta of R. Shimon Bar Yochai* on Exodus, the *Sifri* on Numbers and Deuteronomy, the *Sifra* on Leviticus (also known as *Toras Kohanim*), the *Tosefta of R. Chiya, Osios D'Rabbi Akiva, Avos D'Rabbi Nosson* and the minor tractates of the Talmud.

Ben Ish Chai (R. Yosef Chaim Ben Eliyahu of Bagdad) (1834–1909): At age seven, R. Yosef Chaim fell into a well and nearly drowned. Upon recovering, he dedicated himself to a life of Torah, a vow he later fulfilled by becoming Chief Rabbi of Bagdad and the greatest Sephardic leader since the "Golden Age" of Spain. His Sabbath sermons were attended by thousands, and his rulings were accepted as authoritative throughout the Middle East. Said to have been taught the secrets of Torah by the Prophet Elijah, R. Yosef Chaim was a master Kabbalist who maintained a correspondence with the leaders of the Beth El Yeshiva in Jerusalem. His love of the common folk earned him the appellation of the "Sephardic Baal Shem Tov." R. Yosef Chaim's many works include *Ben Ish Chai: Halachos, Ben Yehoyadah on Ein Yaakov, Rav Pa'alim* (responsa), commentaries on the Five Megillos, and the *Siddur Tefilat Yesharim.*

Berlin, R. Naftali Zvi (1817–1896): Author of *Ha'amek Davar,* a commentary on the Torah, the Netziv (the acronym by which he is best known) was a paragon of the Lithuanian Torah scholar. He succeeded his father-in-law as head of the illustrious Yeshiva of Volozhin, one of Lithuania's greatest Torah centers. There the Netziv taught for over forty years, until a czarist decree to introduce secular subjects to the traditional curriculum led him to close the Yeshiva's doors.

Breslov, R. Nachman of (1772–1810): A great-grandson of the Baal Shem Tov (founder of the Chasidic movement), R. Nachman was one of the most profound and creative figures in Jewish history. Uncompromising in his dedication to the integrity of the Jewish people and Torah tradition, R. Nachman was, at the same time, a universal teacher. He especially encouraged the practice of *hisbodedus*—going to a secluded place, preferably late at night, and speaking to God in one's own language. His writings, while deeply mystical, delineate a highly practical, step-by-step approach to Divine service. Transcribed by his foremost disciple, R. Nosson Sternhartz (q.v.), they include his masterwork, *Likkutei Moharan; Sichos HaRan; Chayei Moharan; Sefer HaMidos* (aphorisms); and *Sippurei Maasios* (stories). Most of these works have been translated to English by the Breslov Research Institute.

Unique among Chasidic sects, the Breslover Chasidim have not only persisted but grown stronger after their master's death. More than six thousand Breslover Chasidim make the yearly pilgrimage to his gravesite in Uman, Ukraine, for the holiday of Rosh Hashanah (the Jewish New Year). Although there are Breslover Chasidim all over the world, the centers of this community are in Israel.

Chofetz Chaim (R. Yisrael Meir HaKohen) (1839–1933): R. Yisrael Meir is best known as the Chafetz Chaim because of his classic work of the same name on the laws of guarding one's speech. One of the most saintly figures in modern times, the Chofetz Chaim was not only an example of piety and virtue, but he actively devoted himself to the spiritual plight of the Jewish people. His masterpiece, the *Mishna Berurah*, clarifies the areas of Torah law most relevant to everyday life. He also authored *Machaneh Yisrael* for Jewish soldiers, *Nid'chei Yisrael* for immigrants struggling to maintain their faith, *Ahavas Chesed* on charity and loans, and a volume on honesty in business. A *kohen* (member of the priest-caste) who fervently awaited the advent of the Messiah, he wrote *Likkutei Halachos*, a compendium of the laws concerning the Holy Temple, and *Tzipisah L'Yeshuah*, a tract on belief in the Redemption.

Cordovero, R. Moshe (1522–1570): After studying the Talmud and legal codes under R. Yosef Karo (q.v.), R. Moshe Cordovero received the newly established *Semichah* (rabbinic ordination) from R. Yaakov bei Rav. He also studied the Kabbalah under R. Shlomo Alkabetz, whom he succeeded as the foremost Kabbalist of Safed prior to the Ari z"l. His best known works are *Pardes Rimmonim*, a masterful summation of virtually all Kabbalistic knowledge extant; *Tomer Devorah*, an ethical work based on Kabbalistic doctrines; *Ohr Ne'erav*, an introduction to the Kabbalah; *Elimah Rabasi* and *Shiur Komah*, two profound Kabbalistic treatises; and *Ohr Yakar* on the *Zohar* and *Sefer Yetzirah*, which have only recently been published. His disciples include R.

Eliyahu de Vidas, author of *Reishis Chochmah*, and R. Menachem Azariah of Fano.

Coucy, R. Moshe of (early thirteenth century): A gifted orator, R. Moshe traveled through Provence and Spain in 1236, addressing the masses and strengthening matters of religious observance. In 1240 he served on the delegation headed by R. Yechiel of Paris to defend the Talmud against accusations that it contained blasphemies against Christianity. His greatest work was the *Sefer Mitzvos Gadol* (best known as the SeMaG). This text delineates the 613 Torah commandments and details their practical implications, based on earlier works, especially those of the Baalei Tosefos (q.v.) and Maimonides (q.v.). The SeMaG was the main legal code studied in European academies until the advent of the *Shulchan Aruch* in the late sixteenth century. R. Moshe's writings include a commentary on the *Chumash* and portions of the *Tosefos* on the Talmud. He also authored *Tosefos Yeshanim* on the Talmudic tractate *Yoma*.

David, Metzudas (R. Yechiel Hillel Ben David Altschuller) (eighteenth century): In order to promote the study of the books of the Prophets, Rabbi David Altschuller began to write a simple commentary on them. This project was edited and completed by his son, R. Yechiel Hillel, who published the entire work in 1770. One part, entitled *Metzudas Zion*, explains individual words. Another part, *Metzudas David*, explains the text. These commentaries are included in almost every edition of the Prophets and Writings.

Dessler, R. Eliyahu (1891–1954): One of the foremost teachers of the Mussar movement, R. Dessler eventually became director of the Kollel in England's famous Gateshead Yeshiva. In 1947 he became Mashgiach of Ponievez Yeshiva in Bnei Brak, Israel, where he remained until his death. R. Dessler's collected talks, *Michtav M'Eliyahu*, reflects a harmonious blend of Mussar, Kabbalah, and Chasidic philosophy, presented in a warm, down-to-earth manner.

Emden, R. Yaakov (1698–1776): Son of the Chacham Zvi, R. Yaakov Emden is best known for his voluminous commentary on the *Siddur* (prayerbook), as well as his responsa, *Sha'alos U'Teshuvos Yaavetz*, and *Mor U'Ketziah*, novellae on *Shulchan Aruch, Orach Chaim*. He also authored a commentary on the Torah, Prophets, and Writings, which is now being reprinted.

Feinstein, R. Moshe (1895–1986): Known by the unassuming title of "Reb Moshe," he was for many decades America's foremost rabbinic authority, as well as Dean of Mesivta Tiferes Jerusalem on New York's Lower East Side. Rabbi Feinstein was born in Russia to a prominent rabbinic family and served as rabbi of Luban, Lithuania, until Communist persecution forced him to emigrate to America in 1937. As a master of Torah law, R. Feinstein dealt with the most difficult contemporary issues; as a master of human nature, he remained accessible not only to his students but to the simple masses of Jewry. His responsa were published as *Igros Moshe*; other works include *Dibros Moshe* (Talmudic novellae), *Kol Ram* (Torah discourses), and an English collection of sermons on the weekly Torah readings, *Bastion of Faith*.

Finkel, R. Nosson Zvi (1849–1928): Known as the Alter ("elder") of Slobodka, R. Nosson Zvi established one of the most influential yeshivos in Lithuania to promulgate the teachings of Mussar. The Alter's approach stressed the essential greatness of man, which is God-given. It is up to the individual to actualize this potential. Although he did not submit his writings for publication, a number of his talks appear in the Mussar anthology, *Chochmas HaMitzvon*. His disciples went on to establish many of America's major Torah institutions.

Ganzfried, R. Shlomo (1804–1886): The head of the *Beis Din* (rabbinical court) of Ungvar, Hungary, R. Ganzfried is best known for his *Kitzur Shulchan Aruch*, a concise version of R. Yosef Karo's standard code of Jewish law, as modified by the rulings of R. Moshe Isserlis and other Ashkenazic authorities. He also authored other legal works, as well as novellae on the Talmud and *Chumash* (Bible).

Gerona, R. Yonah of (1180–1263): A disciple of R. Shlomo of Montpellier and a cousin of Nachmanides (q.v.), Rabbeinu Yonah authored the ethical classic *Shaarei Teshuvah* (*Gates of Repentance*). His other works include glosses on the Rif's *Seder HaHalachos*; several Talmudic commentaries; a commentary on *Pirkei Avos*; *Sefer HaYirah*; and *Igeres HaTeshuvah*. He passed away in Toledo, Spain, while en route to the Holy Land.

HeChasid, R. Yehudah (1150–1217): One of the German *Baalei Tosefos* (q.v.), he is best known for his *Sefer Chasidim*, a classic work of medieval Jewish ethics that weaves together both mysticism and law. R. Yehudah HeChasid received the vast Kabbalistic tradition possessed by his saintly father, R. Shmuel HeChasid. The customs cited in his writings became widely accepted by subsequent generations. Aside from numerous mystical texts, he also wrote religious poetry, including the *Shir HaKavod* (also known as *Anim Zemiros*), with which the Sabbath morning prayer service concludes. Among his many disciples were R. Elazar Rokeach of Worms (author of *Sefer HaRokeach*), R. Yitzchak of Vienna (author of *Ohr Zarua*), and R. Yehudah Ben Kalonymus of Speyer.

HaLevi, R. Yehudah (1080–1145): A disciple of R. Yitzchak Alfasi, who, during his last years, headed the Talmudic academy of Lucena, Spain, R. Yehudah HaLevi is best known as a religious poet and philosopher. His major work, the *Kuzari*, presents the basic tenets of Jewish belief in the form of a dialogue between a Jewish Sage and a gentile king considering conversion. Besides clarifying many philosophical and theological issues, the *Kuzari* reflects the influence of the *Sefer Yetzirah*, a classic text of the Kabbalah. R. Yehudah HaLevi's "*Yom Shabbason*" remains a popular Sabbath table-song, and his lament, "*Zion Halo Sishali*," is recited on the Ninth of Av. In his old age, he fulfilled his dream of traveling to the land of Israel, where he was trampled to death by an Arab horseman while kissing its holy soil.

Hirsch, R. Mendel (1833–1900): The eldest son of R. Samson Raphael Hirsch (q.v.), he followed in his father's footsteps, authoring a commentary for the modern reader on the *Haftoros* (selections from the Prophets read in the synagogue on the Sabbath), the Twelve Prophets, and Lamentations.

Hirsch, R. Samson Raphael (1808–1888): The father of modern German Orthodoxy, R. Hirsch was an inspiring leader, an articulate spokesman for Torah Judaism, and a Talmudic scholar whose brilliance was overshadowed by his many other accomplishments. After becoming Chief Rabbi of Bohemia and Moravia and a member of Parliament, he accepted a less prestigious position in Frankfort-am-Main in order to redress the losses of this former center of Torah to assimilation. His commentaries on the Pentateuch and Psalms are noted for their profound, philosophical approach, addressing the challenges of modern life. *Horeb* is an analysis of the Torah's commandments; *The Nineteen Letters* tackle the questions of the educated youth of his day. R. Hirsch's humanistic theology, although not without precedent, was boldly original in its attempt to forge a meaningful path for the Orthodox Jew living in a secular, egalitarian society.

Horowitz, R. Levi Yitzchak (Bostoner Rebbe) (contemporary): The youngest son of Rabbi Pinchos Dovid Horowitz, founder of the Bostoner dynasty, R. Levi Yitzchak is one of the first Chasidic leaders born in America. After Rabbi Pinchos Dovid's passing in 1946, his oldest son, R. Moshe Horowitz, became the Bostoner Rebbe of New York. Subsequently, R. Levi Yitzchak took his father's position in Boston, establishing the New England Chasidic Center (*Beis Pinchos*) in Brookline and ROFEH to assist those who come to Boston for medical treatments. In 1984, he founded *Givat Pinchas*, a Kollel for Talmudic studies and synagogue, in the Har Nof section of Jerusalem. He now divides his time between Boston and Jerusalem. The Bostoner Rebbe has served on the presidium of Agudath Israel of America and is a member of Israel's Moetzes Gedolei HaTorah.

Ibn Attar, R. Chaim (Ben Moshe) (1696–1743): Born in Sale, Morocco, R. Chaim emigrated to the Holy Land, where he founded an important yeshiva. His disciple, R. Chaim Yosef David Azulai (q.v.), wrote that "whoever beheld his face took him for an angel of God." Moreover, the Baal Shem Tov (q.v.) is reputed to have said that had he and R. Chaim met, they could have brought about the Redemption. *Ohr HaChaim*, his popular commentary on the Torah, expresses many profound Kabbalistic insights in a way that can be grasped by the uninitiated.

Ibn Ezra, R. Avraham (approx. 1080–1164): Born in Toledo, Spain, R. Avraham was not only a major Torah scholar but an expert in grammar, poetry, philosophy, astronomy, and medicine. He was an intimate friend of R. Yehudah HaLevi (q.v.), author of the *Kuzari*. Most of his works were written after the age of sixty, when he lived as a wandering ascetic. R. Avraham Ibn Ezra is best known for his commentary on the books of the Torah and Prophets. His Sabbath tablesong, *"Ki Eshm'rah Shabbat,"* is still popular among Jews of both Middle-Eastern (Sephardic) and European (Ashkenazic) descent.

Kara, MaHari (R. Yosef Ben Shimon) (late eleventh–early twelfth centuries): An older contemporary of Rashi, MaHari Kara lived in Troyes, France. Like his uncle and teacher, R. Menachem Ben Chelbo Kara, he acquired the name Kara (from *Mikra* or Scripture) because of the biblical commentary that was his life's work. Rashi (q.v.) greatly admired MaHari Kara and incorporated some of the latter's suggestions into his own commentaries.

Karo, R. Yosef Ben Ephraim (1488–1575): Author of the classic code of Jewish law, the *Shulchan Aruch*, R. Yosef Karo was born in Toledo, Spain, and fled with his parents to Constantinople during the dread Inquisition. While in Turkey, he began to write the *Beis Yosef*, his monumental commentary on the *Arba Turim*. Upon his arrival in Safed, Israel, in 1535, he was appointed to the *Beis Din* (rabbinical court) of R. Yaakov ben Rav, who attempted to revive the ancient institution of *semichah* (ordination). R. Yosef Karo received this *semicha* from R. Yaakov be Rav and gave it in turn to R. Moshe Alshich and R. Chaim Vital (q.v.), among others. A saintly person of ascetic habits, he studied Kabbalah with Rabbi Shlomo Alkabetz and was visited by a *Maggid* (spirit-teacher), who revealed the mysteries of Torah to him. These teachings were published as *Maggid Mesharim*. R. Yosef Karo's other works include *Kesef Mishneh* on the Rambam, *Sha'alos U'Teshuvos Beis Yosef* (responsa), and commentaries on the Torah, *Pirke Avos*, and the Song of Songs, originally published together in *Ohr Tzaddikim* (Salonika, 1599).

Kimchi, R. David (1160–1235): Born in Provence, R. David Kimchi is best known for his classic commentary on the Bible, of which we possess only the sections on the Prophets, Psalms, Proverbs, Chronicles, and Genesis. His interpretations stress the plain meaning of the text, yet incorporate teachings from the Midrash. An expert grammarian, he also authored the *Sefer Michlol*, which Reuchlin used in order to study Hebrew. His refutations of Christian theology, originally censored, were later published as *Teshuvos HaNotzrim*.

Kook, R. Avraham Yitzchak HaKohen (1865–1935): The first Ashkenazic Chief Rabbi of the Holy Land, R. Kook was a visionary who perceived the return of the Jewish people to their land in Messianic terms. He also saw himself at the interface of tradition and change, exile and redemption. R. Kook was a master of Torah law, as his voluminous responsa demonstrate. Yet he had the soul of a mystic and poet who needed to create his own language and literary genre to express himself. His philosophical works include *Oros, Oros HaTeshuvah, Oros HaKodesh, Arpilei Tohar* and *Ein Ayah* on *Ein Yaakov*; legal works include *Mishpat Kohen, Daas Kohen, Ezras Kohen, Orech Mishpat,* and *Shavas Ha'aretz* on the Sabbatical Year. His views were sometimes opposed by Jerusalem's pre-eminent Torah authority, R. Chaim Sonnenfeld; however, at the personal level, both men maintained the highest respect for one another.

Koretz, R. Pinchas of (early 1700s–1791): When the disciples of the Baal Shem Tov asked who would succeed him, the master replied, "There is a bear in the woods (meaning R. Dov Ber of Mezeritch), and R. Pinchas is a Sage." One of the first Rebbes (Chasidic leaders), R. Pinchas was largely responsible for the rapid spread of Chasidim throughout central Ukraine. Several collections of his teachings have been published, including *Imrei Pinchas* and *Midrash Pinchas*.

Lifshutz, R. Yisrael (1782–1860): Rabbi of Chodsiezen (Kolmar) and, in his later years, Danzig, Germany, he was not only a master of Talmudic law—as evinced by his classic commentary on the Mishna, *Tiferes Yisrael*—but an original thinker who boldly addressed the scientific and philosophical issues of his day. Although many of his works still remain in manuscript, his discourse on the age of the universe has been translated to English by R. Yaakov Elman and published together with R. Aryeh Kaplan's *Immortality, Resurrection and the Age of the Universe* (Ktav 1993).

Lubavitch, R. Dov Ber of (1773–1827): The brilliant son and successor of Rabbi Shneur Zalman of Liadi, R. Dov Ber disseminated the teachings of Chabad Chasidism throughout White Russia and attracted thousands of new disciples. Concerned with the physical plight of the masses, he organized farming communities so that the Jews of Russia might become self-supporting. He also bought land in Hebron and established a yeshiva there. Like his father, he was imprisoned by the czar in 1826 due to slanders from opponents of the Chasidic movement. His works include *Toras Chaim, Sha'arei Orah, Sha'arei Teshuvah, Imrei Binah, Derech Chaim, Ateres Rosh, Poke'ach Ivrim,* and two major tracts on ecstacy and meditative prayer, *Kuntres HaHispa'alus* and *Ner Mitzvah V'Torah Ohr*.

Maharal of Prague (R. Yehudah Loewe Ben Betzalel) (1512–1609): One of the most original and profound thinkers in Jewish history, the Maharal was a descendant of King David. He served as Chief Rabbi of Moravia, residing in Nikolsberg for twenty years. Then, in 1573, he moved his yeshiva to Prague, where he became Chief Rabbi in 1598. Known as a miracle worker, the Maharal became a folk hero (legend credits him with creating a *golem*, a clay giant brought to life by Kabbalistic means, in order to protect the Jews of Prague from pogroms). However, his greatest accomplishment was the formulation of a comprehensive self-contained system of Jewish thought. His works, available as an 18 volume set, include *Gur Aryeh* on the Torah, *Derech Chaim*, *Nesivos Olam, Netzach Yisrael, Be'er HaGolah*, and *Gevuros Hashem*.

Maimonides, R. Avraham (1186–1237): The only son of R. Moses Maimonides, he was educated by his father, whom he succeeded as the Sultan's physician. R. Avraham was the *Naggid*, or leading rabbinic authority, in Egypt; as such, his influence extended over almost the entire Middle East. Although none of his major works have survived in their entirety, we possess several collections of legal responsa, commentaries on Genesis and Exodus, and part of his encyclopedic *Sefer HaMaspik L 'Ovdei Hashem* (*High Ways to Perfection*), which underscores the pietistic and mystical aspects of Judaism. A source of controversy was R. Avraham's affinity with the Moslem Sufis, whom he believed to possess certain traditions of the ancient prophets of Israel.

Maimonides, R. Moses (1135–1204): Born in Cordova, Spain, R. Moses Maimonides was probably the most celebrated Torah scholar of the Sephardic medieval period. He and his family fled to Fez, Morocco, in 1160 due to the persecution of the Moslem Almohades. There Maimonides wrote his commentary on the Mishna. In 1166, he and his family were again forced to flee, this time to Egypt. While serving as personal physician to Saladin, the sultan of Egypt and Syria, Maimonides wrote his classic of Talmudic law, the *Mishneh Torah* (also known as the *Yad Ha-Chazakah*), and the *Moreh Nevuchim* (*Guide for the Perplexed*), which reflects the influence of Aristotle. Despite the controversy surrounding his philosophical works, Maimonides' influence on subsequent generations of Talmudic scholars has been immeasurable.

Malbim, R. Meir Leib (1809–1879): During his youth, the Malbim, as he is commonly known, studied the Kabbalah under the Chasidic master R. Zvi Hirsch Eichenstein of Ziditchov (1763–1831). A relatively obscure communal rabbi, he began to gain recognition with the publication of his commentary on the *Megillah* of Esther in 1845, and subsequently on the remaining books of the Bible. The Malbim's works are now counted among the most important commentaries on the Prophets since the classics of the medieval period. He also authored legal treatises, including *Artzos HaChaim* on the *Shulchan Aruch*.

Meiri, R. Menachem (1249–1306): R. Menachem Meiri lived in Provence at the end of the period of the *Baalei Tosefos* (q.v.). His encyclopedic commentary on the Talmud, *Beis HaBechirah*, is a masterpiece of lucidity, most of which only existed in manuscript until recent times. *Chiddushei HaMeiri*, a collection of Talmudic novellae, *Chibbur HaTeshuvah* on repentance, and some of his legal works are also extant. Of his writings on *Tanach*, commentaries on Psalms and Proverbs are all that have survived.

Midrash: These nonlegalistic teachings of the rabbis of the Talmudic era explore events and issues in the Torah, expressing a wide range of ideas and opinions of both a practical and philosophical nature. Major collections include the *Midrash Rabbah, Midrash Tanchumah, Pirke D'Rabbi Eliezer, Midrash Shochar Tov, Midrash Lekach Tov, Midrash Talpios*, and *Yalkut Shimoni*.

Mishna: Organized and edited by Rabbi Yehudah HaNasi in the second century B.C.E., the Mishna comprises the foundation of the Oral Law. Its six orders discuss the laws of agriculture, religious festivals and practices, marriage and divorce, civil law, the sacrificial services, and ritual purity. The tractate *Avos* (*Chapters of the Fathers*) is unique in that it departs from matters of law to present a sampling of the ethical teachings and wisdom of the Sages.

Munk, R. Elie (1900–1987): Born in Paris to a prominent rabbinic family, R. Elie Munk was deeply influenced by the thought of R. Samson Raphael Hirsch (q.v.) and the Kabbalistic teachings of R. Moshe Cordovero (q.v.). He authored numerous works directed to the broad spectrum of the Jewish people, including *The World of Prayer, Social Justice and Israel, Ascent to Harmony*, and a biblical commentary, *The Call of the Torah*.

Mussar ("Reproof"): Founded by Rabbi Yisrael Salanter (q.v.) in the early nineteenth century, the Mussar movement sought to bring about a spiritual transformation of the individual through intensive self-examination, the cultivation of positive character traits, and the study of pietistic texts such as *Orchos Tzaddikim, Mesilas Yesharim, Chovos HaLevavos*, and *Shaarei Teshuvah*. Although Rabbi Salanter's path initially met with intense opposition, it eventually had a profound effect on the Lithuanian yeshiva system.

Nachmanides (R. Moshe Ben Nachman) (1194–1270): The foremost Torah scholar of Spain of his generation, Nachmanides was a disciple of R. Yehudah ben Yakar and R. Nosson ben Meir of Trinquetaille and studied Kabbalah under R. Azriel and R. Ezra of Gerona. His classic commentary on the *Chumash* (Five Books of Moses) is unique in that it not only interprets the verses, but analyzes topics, often on more than one level. He also authored *Shaar HaGemul* on Divine judgement and the resurrection of the dead, *Sefer HaGe'ulah* on the coming of the Messiah, brilliant novellae on the Talmud, and various tracts on matters of Jewish law. Ordered to debate a Jewish apostate by King James of Aragon, his refutations of Christianity (preserved in *Sefer HaViku'ach*) were so devastating that he was expelled from the country. At age seventy-two, Nachmanides emigrated to the Holy Land, arriving in Acco in 1267. During his last years, he established a circle of disciples in Jerusalem, which led to the community's physical and spiritual revival. He is buried in Hebron near the Cave of Machpelah.

Rashi (acronym for **Rabbi Shlomo Yitzchaki**) (1040–1105): Scion of a prominent rabbinic family that traced its roots through Rabbi Yochanan HaSandlar to King David, Rashi is considered the pre-eminent commentator on both the *Chumash* (Five Books of Moses) and the Talmud. Over two hundred commentaries have been written on the former work, and the latter is considered indispensable to the study of the Talmud. A testimony to the greatness of these works is the statement of Chasidic master, R. Nachman of Breslov (q.v.) that "Rashi is the brother of the holy Torah" (*Sichos HaRan* 223). Born in Troyes, France, he traveled to Mainz and Worms, where he studied under disciples of Rabbi Gershom Meor HaGolah. Returning to his native city in 1065, he refused to accept a rabbinic position but, instead, became a wine merchant. Nevertheless, a circle of gifted disciples formed around Rashi. This school persisted for two hundred years through the *Baalei Tosefos* (q.v.).

Rivkah's, R. Moshe (1595–1671): R. Moshe Rivkah's was a prominent scholar in Vilna until the Cossacks invaded the city in 1655, forcing many inhabitants to flee. He resettled in Amsterdam, where he authored his classic *Be'er HaGolah* on *Shulchan Aruch*, as well as *Klalei HaHora'ah*, a guidebook for rendering decisions in Jewish law, and a commentary on the entire Mishna; however, the latter two works were never published. Despite the great respect he enjoyed in Amsterdam, R. Moshe longed to return to Vilna, and succeeded in doing so before his death. His illustrious descendant, the Vilna Gaon, frequently cites the *Be'er HaGolah* in his own writings on *Shulchan Aruch*.

Rogotchov, R. Yosef Rosen of (1858–1936): One of the most brilliant Talmudic scholars of the modern era, the "Rogotchover Gaon," as he is commonly known, was a Chasid of the Kapust branch of Chabad. However, he studied under the Lithuanian giants, R. Yehoshua Leib Diskin (Brisker Rav of Jerusalem) and R.

Yosef Dov Soloveitchik (Beis HaLevi), who arranged for him to be the study-partner of his son, R. Chaim Soloveitchik of Brisk. His detailed knowledge of every facet of Torah was legendary. Moreover, he developed a unique system of thought, based on Maimonides, in which every issue is understood in its ultimate legal context. Although numerous manuscripts on various tractates of the Talmud remain unpublished, the Rogotchover Gaon's _Tsafnas Pane'ach_ on Rambam, _Tsafnas Pane'ach_ on _Chumash_, and _Teshuvos Tsafnas Pane'ach_ are available.

Sacks, R. Jonathan (contemporary): The present Chief Rabbi of England, Rabbi Sacks has been principal of Jews' College, London, visiting professor of philosophy at the University of London, and rabbi of the Golders Green and Marble Arches synagogues. Noted for their intellectual verve, his books include _Tradition in an Untraditional Age_ and _Arguments for the Sake of Heaven_. R. Sacks has also translated a volume of discourses by the late Lubavitcher Rebbe (q.v.), written numerous scholarly articles, and is the editor of _L'Eylah: A Journal of Judaism Today_.

Salanter, R. Yisrael (1810–1883): Founder of the modern Mussar movement, he reinfused generations of Talmudic scholars (particularly in his native Lithuania) with the loftiest spiritual and ethical ideals. "It is easier to learn through the entire Talmud," he said, "than to correct a single bad character trait." His teachings have been published as _Ohr Yisrael_ and _Koch'vei Ohr_. Inasmuch as R. Salanter did not write down his discourses, these works consist largely of letters to his disciple, R. Yitzchak Blazer (d. 1907). Although initially rejected, the Mussar movement eventually overcame its opponents and remains influential today.

Schneerson, R. Menachem Mendel (1902–1994): The seventh leader of the Chabad-Lubavitch movement, R. Schneerson was a direct descendant of R. Shneur Zalman of Liadi and a son-in-law of the previous leader, R. Yosef Yitzchak. A master of both Talmudic law and Chasidic philosophy, he also studied the sciences at the University of Berlin and the Sorbonne. Assuming leadership of the Lubavitcher Chasidim after his father-in-law's passing in 1950, he spearheaded an outreach movement of a scope unprecedented in Jewish history. His *Likkutei Sichos* (collected talks), *Maamarim* (Chasidic discourses), and letters discuss virtually every major issue in the Torah, while boldly addressing contemporary political and scientific issues, as well as the problems of everyday life. In his last years, the Lubavitcher Rebbe used to spend entire Sundays giving out dollars to the thousands who streamed to his door in order to inspire the giving of more charity and thus hasten the Messianic Redemption.

Sforno, R. Ovadyah (1470–1550): One of the outstanding Jewish thinkers of the Italian Renaissance, R. Ovadyah Sforno was both a Torah scholar and physician. While living in Rome, he befriended the Christian humanist Johann Reuchlin and taught him Hebrew. He later settled in Bologna, where, in addition to continuing his medical practice, he served as head of the local rabbinical court. Most famous for his commentary on the Torah, R. Ovadyah Sforno's many works include commentaries on the Song of Songs, Ecclesiastes, Job, Psalms, Jonah, Habbakuk, Zechariah, *Pirkei Avos*, and a defense of the Torah entitled *Ohr Amim*. He prepared a Latin translation of the latter work for his admirer, King Henri II of France.

Soloveitchik, R. Ahron (contemporary): A descendant of the innovative Lithuanian talmudist Rabbi Chaim of Brisk, R. Ahron Soloveitchik has been one of America's foremost rabbinic leaders for more than half a century. Together with his late brother, R. Joseph Ber Soloveitchik, he guided generations of Talmud students in Yeshivah University's Rabbi Yitzchak Elchanan Seminary. In 1974 he founded Yeshivas Brisk of Chicago. Despite the debilitating stroke he suffered in 1983, R. Soloveitchik still lectures in both rabbinical colleges.

Sternhartz, R. Nosson (1780–1844): The foremost disciple of Rabbi Nachman of Breslov (q.v.), R. Nosson transcribed and published his master's teachings and continued to lead the

Breslover Chasidic community after R. Nachman's untimely death. His own collected discourses, based on *Likkutei Moharan*, are entitled *Likkutei Halachos*. This eight-volume work is a unique tapestry of Talmud, Midrash, Mussar, Kabbalah, Chasidic wisdom, and homespun advice on the problems of everyday life. R. Nosson's prayers, also based on *Likkutei Moharan*, are published as *Likkutei Tefillos* (*The Fiftieth Gate*, in English translation by Avraham Greenbaum).

Talmud: The collected oral traditions, Torah interpretations, and wisdom of the Sages of Israel that forms the basis of rabbinic law and normative Jewish religious practice. A unique work that encompasses everything from biology to metaphysics, the Talmud primarily discusses and debates issues found in the Mishna (q.v.). The Babylonian Talmud was redacted in its present form by Ravina and Rav Ashi in approximately 505 c.e. The Jerusalem Talmud was redacted by Rabbi Yochanan Bar Nafcha in the third century c.e. and finalized several generations later.

Tiferes Yisrael: (see Lifshutz, R. Yisrael)

Torah: The Five Books of Moses; sometimes denotes the entire corpus of Jewish religious teachings.

Tosefos (or *Baalei Tosefos*; "Additions"): A collection of analytical discussions on the Talmud by the school of Rashi (q.v.) during the twelfth to fourteenth centuries in France and Germany. Outstanding among them were Rashi's grandsons, Rashbam and Rabbeinu Tam. The glosses of *Tosefos* are printed in all major editions of the Talmud, opposite the commentary of Rashi.

Tosefos Yom Tov (R. Yom Tov Lipman Heller) (1579–1654): Born in Wallerstein, Bavaria, R. Yom Tov traveled to Praque to study under the famous Maharal (q.v.) and R. Ephraim Lunshitz. As Chief Rabbi of Prague, he was accused of making statements against Christianity in his writings and condemned to death. After receiving a royal pardon, he left Austria and served as rabbi of several communities in Poland. He spent his last years in

Cracow. *Tosefos Yom Tov* is the title of his most famous work, a commentary on the Mishna.

Ujheli, R. Moshe Teitelbaum of (1759–1841): A childhood prodigy, R. Moshe did not become a disciple of R. Yaakov Yitzchak, the Chozeh ("Seer") of Lublin, until the age of forty. Prior to that he served as communal rabbi of Shiniva, Galicia, and was a scholar of repute, who regularly corresponded with the Chasam Sofer. During his later years, he was instrumental in bringing the teachings of Chasidim to Hungary, where he also became known as a miracle worker. The prominent dynasties of Satmar and Sighet are numbered among R. Moshe's descendants. His major works include *Heishiv Moshe* (responsa) and *Yismach Moshe* (Chasidic sermons on the weekly Torah portion).

Vilna, R. Pinchas Eliyahu of (eighteenth century): One of the major proponents of Lurianic Kabbalah, R. Pinchas Eliyahu authored *Ta'im Eitzah*, an important commentary on *Mishnas Chasidim*, which summarizes and distills the key teachings of the Ari z"l. However, he is best known for his encyclopedic *Sefer HaBris*, a guide to the attainment of *Ruach HaKodesh* (enlightenment) based on R. Chaim Vital's *Shaarei Kedushah*. This work, which discusses everything from metaphysics to meditation, also attempts to reconcile Kabbalistic doctrine with the scientific theories of the day.

Vital, R. Chaim (1543–1620): The foremost disciple of master Kabbalist Rabbi Yitzchak Luria (the Ari z"l), R. Chaim transcribed and edited the authoritative versions of his teacher's works and wrote numerous books of his own. His *Shaarei Kedushah* is both an introduction to Kabbalah and a guide to the attainment of *Ruach HaKodesh* (enlightenment). A diary of his dreams and visions was originally published as *Shivchei R. Chaim Vital* (Ostrog 1826) and subsequently as *Sefer HaChezyonos* (Jerusalem 1954). Ordained by R. Yosef Karo (q.v.), his legal responsa are included with those of his son, Rabbi Shmuel Vital, in *Teshuvos Be'er Mayim Chaim*.

Yaivi, Rav (acronym for **R. Yaakov Yosef of Ostrog**) (1738–1791): A close disciple of the Maggid of Mezeritch, R. Yaakov Yosef of Ostrog was especially dedicated to the poor, whose lot he shared. He also spoke out against the appointment of rabbis to communal positions for reasons other than their scholarship and personal qualifications. His writings include *Moreh Mikdash*, on synagogue decorum, and *Rav Yaivi*, a Chasidic work.

Zohar Chadash: "New Zohar," so called because it was first published in the late sixteenth century, some three hundred years after the main text of the *Zohar* was made public. Preserved by the Safed Kabbalists, these writings are portions of the original work, which often complete sections that break off in the middle.

Zohar: One of the fundamental texts of Kabbalah, the *Zohar* contains the mystical teachings of the Talmudic Sage Rabbi Shimon Bar Yohai, as compiled by Rabbi Abba and his colleagues. According to tradition, these writings were preserved in secrecy until the thirteenth century, when they were revealed by Rabbi Moshe de Leon.

Related Reading

Bindman, Y. (1995). *The Seven Colors of the Rainbow.* San Jose, CA: Resource Publications Inc.

Davis, J.D. (1996). *Finding the God of Noah.* Hoboken, NJ: Ktav.

HaKohen, Y. (1995). *The Universal Jew.* Jerusalem/New York: Feldheim.

Hanke, K. (1996). *Turning to Torah: The Emerging Noachide Movement.* Northvale, NJ: Jason Aronson.

Hirsch, S.R. (1980). *The Pentateuch.* New York: Judaica Press.

———. (1976). *Judaism Eternal.* London/New York: Soncino Press.

Lichtenstein, A. (1981). *The Seven Laws of Noah.* New York: Berman Books.

Luria, M. (1994). *Elijah Benamozegh: Israel and Humanity.* Mahwah, NJ: Paulist Press.

Munk, E. (1987). *Ascent to Harmony.* Jerusalem/New York: Feldheim.

Index

Aaron, 70

Abraham
circumcision, 143
discovery of God, 171
Divine promise, 117
Ishmael, 86–87
as parent of converts, 114, 143
as patriarch, 36, 157
People of Abraham, 126

Adam, 165–166

Adam (man), term used in Torah, 131–136

Adjudication, of non-Jews, 62

Aleinu prayer, 74, 75, 189

Alter, Rabbi Yehudah Aryeh Leib, 199

Alter of Slobodka (Rabbi Nosson Zvi Finkel), 204

Am segula, 138, 139

Animal slaughter, 170

Anointing, 146–147

Anti-Semites, Chosen People concept, 111

Ark of the Covenant, 115

Assimilation, 107

Atonement, 115, 119

Azkari, Rabbi Elazar, 199

Azulai, Rabbi Chaim David Yosef, 199–200

Baal Shem Tov, 200

Bachaye, Rabbeinu (Bachya), 200

Baraisa, 200

Barbarian, defined, 52–53

Ben Ish Chai (Rabbi Yosef Chaim Ben Eliyahu of Bagdad), 200–201

Berlin, Rabbi Naftali Zvi, 201

Bitul, 147

Blasphemy, 82, 167–168

Bondage, 22

Book of the Upright, 35–36

Bostoner Rebbe (Rabbi Levi
    Yitzchak Horowitz),
    206–207
Breslov, Rabbi Nachman of,
    190, 201–202
Brotherhood, 139–140
Business
    buying stolen goods, 44
    fairness toward employees,
        49
    honesty in, 41–46, 50–51,
        52–53

Charity, 172–173
Chasid, term used in Torah,
    176–177
Chasidic teachings, for Non-
    Jews, 105
Cheating, 38, 50
Chida (Rabbi Azulai),
    199–200
Children, of converts, 67
Choeftez Chaim (Rabbi Yisrael
    Meir HaKohen), 202
Chosen People, 111–145
Christians, 90–92, 111
Citizenship, 37–40
Civilization, well-being of,
    39–40
Commandments, obeying, 15
Compassion, divine, 23–25
Consuming live flesh, Seven
    Universal Laws of Noah,
    170
Contemplation, 171

Conversion, coming of the
    Messiah, 91
Converts
    Abraham as parent of con-
        verts, 114, 143
    Maimonides' letter to
        Obadiah, 71–73
    marriage to, 67
    proselytization, 74–76
    righteous proselytes, 63–69,
        71–73
Cordovero, Rabbi Moshe,
    202–203
Coucy, Rabbi Moshe of, 203
Covenant, 154
Creation, purpose of, 112–113
Creatures
    love of all, 3, 9, 17, 29–30
    peace among, 27
Crown
    of kingship, 59
    of priesthood, 59
    of Torah, 59–62
Cruelty, 22
Customers, fairness to, 50

Daughters of Jerusalem, 81
David, Metzudas (Rabbi
        Yechiel Hillel Ben David
        Altschuller), 203
David (King), 115, 154
Deceitfulness to, 42–43
Dessler, Rabbi Eliyahu, 203
Dialogue, prayer for, 193–194
Discrimination, 19

Dishonesty, 38, 41–46, 48, 50
Dispersion, nations of the world, 99
Divine forgiveness, 120
Divine image, 4, 6, 11, 124, 125, 132, 144, 168
Divine justice, 54
Divine mercy, 173
Divine Oneness, 68, 84, 96, 114, 156, 166, 168, 181, 185–186
Divine service, 102
Divine understanding, 10
Divine wisdom, 10
Divine witness, Transgression, 118

Eating live flesh, Seven Universal Laws of Noah, 170
Eisek, 24
Eliezer, 86, 87
Elijah the Prophet, 29, 32, 47, 83
Embezzlement, 44
Emden, Rabbi Yaakov, 204
Employees, fairness to, 49
Enlightenment
    Messianic era, 145
    non-Jews, 83–85
Equality, 19
Esau, 90
Ethics, 97, 108
Evil, punishment for, 130

Exile, 63, 78, 85, 116
    and redemption, 98–99, 179
Ezekiel, 127
Ezra, 116

Fairness, 38
    to customers, 50
    to employees, 49
Family of Man, 11–12
Fear, of God, 184–185
Feinstein, Rabbi Moshe, 204
Fellow travelers, 4, 16
Festival of Booths, *see* Sukkos
Finkel, Rabbi Nosson Zvi (Alter of Slobodka), 204
Flattery, 42–43
Forgiveness, 120
Freedom, 22
Freedom of choice, 112, 177

Ganzfried, Rabbi Shlomo, 204–205
Genesis, Book of, Book of the Upright, 35–36
Gentiles, *see* Non-Jews
Gerone, Rabbi Yonah of, 205
God
    attributes, *see under* Divine
    children of, 144
    contemplation of, 171
    dedication to, 112, 137
    Divine service, 102
    as divine witness, 118
    fear of, 184–185
    forgiveness, 120

God (*continued*)
   image of, 4, 6, 11, 124, 125,
      132, 144, 168
   Jews' mission, 96–97, 107
   knowing God, 83–85
   Oneness of, 68, 84, 96, 114,
      156, 166, 168, 181,
      185–186
   peace in the world, 32
   prayer, *see also* Prayer
   purpose of creation,
      112–113
   return to, 100–101, 173
   speech to call out to, 94,
      95
   suffering of Israel, 122–123
   as sustainer of all, 26
   unity in diversity, 141
Good citizenship, 37–40
Good deeds, 172–173
Government, prayer for, 37–
   38, 176
Grace after meals, 26

HaLevi, Rabbi Yehudah,
   205–206
Harmony, universal, 109–110
Hatred of mankind, 40
Healing the World (*Tikkun
   olam*), 93–97, 113
HeChasid, Rabbi Yehudah,
   205
High Priest (*Kohan Gadol*), 59,
   60, 66, 70, 135
Hillel, 197

Hirsch, Rabbi Mendel, 206
Hirsch, Rabbi Samson Raphael,
   206
Holy nation, 124
Holy Temple, 78, 79, 115–
   116, 170, 172
Honesty, in business, 41–46,
   50–51, 52–53
Honoring father and mother,
   15
Horowitz, Rabbi Levi Yitzchak
   (Bostoner Rebbe),
   206–207
Human nature, 146, 167
Humility, 147, 148

Ibn Attar, Rabbi Chaim (Ben
   Moshe), 207
Ibn Ezra, Rabbi Avraham, 207
Idolatry, Seven Universal Laws
   of Noah, 168
Idol-worshipper, lesson from,
   15
Image of God, 4, 6, 11, 124,
   125, 132, 144, 168
Immorality, Seven Universal
   Laws of Noah, 169–170
Injustice, Moses and, 20–21
Isaac, as patriarch, 36
Isaiah, 148
Ishmael, 86–87, 90
Islam, 87, 90–92
Israel, 101
   advantage over other nations,
      133–134

am segula, 138, 139
called *adam*, 131–136
ethics and, 108
families of the workd, 127
as heart of the world, 120
Holy Temple, 78, 79
Jerusalem, 79–89
light to all nations, 105,
    159–161, 184
love of God, 121
mission, 127
non-Jews in, 88–89
purpose of, 142–143
suffering of, 122–123, 150
Issachar, 103

Jacob, 36, 90, 101
Jeremiah, 104
Jerusalem, 79–82, 155
Jeshurun, 101
Jesus, 91
Jethro, 67, 68, 94, 129
Jews
    assimilation, 107
    bearers of God's word, 142
    as Chosen People, 111–145
    history, 113–117
    joyfulness, 173–174
    mission and purpose of,
        96–97, 107, 119,
        137, 142
    nationalism, 143
    as People of Abraham, 126
    segregation of, 107
Jonah, 93

Joy, in Judaism, 173–174
Justice
    cosmic, 54
    Moses and, 20–21
    Seven Universal Laws of
        Noah, 167
    uniform standard, 53

Kadosh (holy), 137
Kara, MaHari (Rabbi Yosef Ben
    Shimon), 207
Karo, Rabbi Yosef Ben
    Ephraim, 207–208
Kidnapping, Seven Universal
    Laws of Noah, 169
Killing, 168–169
Kimchi, Rabbi David, 208
King, non-Jewish, 38
King Solomon's Prayer, 77
Knowledge, as redemption, 85
Kohanim (priests), 45, 55, 59
    Israel as nation of, 81
    Jews as, 125, 127
    origin of, 70
    righteous converts, 64
Kohen Gadol (High Priest), 59,
    60, 66, 70, 135
Kook, Rabbi Avraham Yitzchak
    HaKohen, 208–209
Koretz, Rabbi Pinchas of, 209

Languages, 57, 81, 91, 94, 95
Law, of local government, 38
Lifshutz, Rabbi Yisrael, 209

Light to all the nations, 105, 159–161, 184
Likkutei Tefillos, 190
Live flesh, consuming, 170
Love
  of all creatures, 3, 9, 17, 29–30
  thy neighbor, 6–9
Lower Unification, 185, 186
Loyalty, to country of citizenship, 38
Lubavitch, Rabbi Dov Ber of, 209

Maharal of Prague (Rabbi Yehudah Loewe Ben Betzalel), 210
Maimonides, 71–73, 97, 104, 210–211
Malbim, Rabbi Meir Leib, 211
Man
  brotherhood of, 139–140
  dedication to, 142–144
  family of man, 11–12
  fellow travelers, 4, 16
  freedom for all, 22
  hatred of, 40
  human nature, 146, 167
  image of God, 4, 6, 11, 124, 125, 132
  love all creatures, 3, 9, 17
  as neighbor, 6–9
  racial equality, 19
Manna, 26
Marriage, to a convert, 67
Matriarchs, 114–115

Meditation, 171
Meiri, Rabbi Menachem, 211
Mercy, 23–25
Messiah, 34
  anointing, 146–147
  judgment by, 148–149
  peace unto the nations, 159
  Peleh Yo-etz, 149
  recognizing, 151
  self-effacement, 147
  tasks, 150–151
  wisdom of, 146–147
Messianic era, 91, 92, 97, 98–99
  efforts to bring, 105
  enlightenment, 145
  existential distress and, 145
  joy, 174
  peace, 145, 153, 159
  Torah in, 180
  wealth, 149
Messianic vision, 145–161
Midrash, 211
Mishna, 211–212
Mishpat, 53
Moab, 23
Mohammed, 91
Morality, 97, 109–110, 113
Moses, 68–70, 71, 73
  as incarnation of Noah, 113
  Jethro's wisdom, 129
  as social activist, 20–21
Moslems, 90–92
Mount Sinai, Holy Temple and, 115

Munk, Rabbi Elie, 212
Murder, Seven Universal Laws
    of Noah, 168–169
Mussar, 212

Nachman of Breslov, Rabbi,
    190, 201–202
Nachmanides (Rabbi Moshe
    ben Nachman), 212–213
Nationalism, Jews, 143
Nations
    all nations are beloved, 124
    am segula, 138, 139
    dispersion, 99
    gather in Jerusalem, 80
    harmony with Israel,
        109–110
    holy nation, 124
    Jews as model for, 126
    light to all nations, 105,
        159–161
    one united kingdom of
        God, 141
    origin of, 113
    pure speech, 94
    sing to God, 156–157
    superiority over Israel, 133
    wars between, 34
    wisdom of, 2
Nature, 128
Neighbor, love of, 6–9
Nineveh, 23
Noah
    belief in God, 114
    incarnation as Moses, 113

righteousness, 114
Seven Universal Laws, *see*
    Seven Universal Laws
    of Noah
Non-Jews
    adjudication of, 62
    blessings of, 13–14
    burying their dead, 29, 31
    caring for their sick, 29, 31
    Chasidic teachings for, 105
    converts, 63–69
    as customers, 50
    deceitfulness to, 42–43
    divine compassion for,
        23–25
    as employees, 49
    Enlightenment, 83–85
    greeting, 30–31
    in the Holy Land, 86–89
    Holy Temple, 78
    in image of God, 12, 132
    injustice not permitted, 20,
        21
    Jerusalem, 80–82
    King Solomon's Prayer, 77
    Messianic era, 91, 92, 98–99
    morality, 109–110
    other religions, 90–92
    preventing transgressions by,
        93
    respect for, 1–5, 7, 12
    righteousness, 41, 55–58,
        61, 131–132
    righteous proselytes, 63–69,
        71–73

Non-Jews (*continued*)
  royalty, 38
  Sabbatical Year work, 30
  Seven Universal Laws of
    Noah, 45, 58, 61, 62,
    103, 104, 105, 112
  stealing from, 41–45, 48
  tefillin, 183–184
  Torah distinction from Jew,
    19
  Torah study by, 59–60, 171

Obadiah, Maimonides' letter
  to, 71–73
Oneness of God, 68, 84, 96,
  114, 156, 166, 168, 181,
  185–186

Passover, 24, 101
Patriarchs, 35–36, 114–115,
  157
Peace, 27–34
  Messianic era, 145, 153,
    159
  paths of, 27–34
  prayer for, 32–33, 37, 194
Peleh Yo-etz, 149
Penitents, 68
People of Abraham, 126
Perfecting the World (*Tikkun*
  olam), 93–97, 113
Prayer
  Aleinu, 74, 75, 189
  for government, 37–38,
    176

for hidden *tzaddikim*,
  194–196
King Solomon's Prayer, 77
for peaceful dialogue,
  193–194
peace results from, 32–33,
  37, 194
putting on *tefillin*, 186–186
Rabbi Nosson's prayers, 190,
  193–194
relationship with God, 172
Rosh Hashanah, 189–192
for Sabbath, 196
for unity in diversity, 194
universal brotherhood, 139
Priests, *see Kohanim*
Proselytes
  Maimonides' letter to
    Obadiah, 71–73
  righteous proselytes, 63–69,
    71–73
  seeking, 74–76
Punishment, for transgression,
  130
Pure language, 95
Pure speech, 94

"Quarrelsome tongues," 57–58
Queen, non-Jewish, 38

Racial equality, 19
Rashi (Rabbi Shlomo Yitzchaki),
  213
Rechovos, 24

Redemption
  by Messiah, 150
  exile and, 98–99, 179
  knowledge as, 85
  Messianic era, 155
Religions, 90–92
Repairing the World (*Tikkun
    olam*), 93–97, 113
Respect, non-Jews and Jews,
    1–5, 7, 12
Restitution, for theft, 41, 169
Return to God, 100–101
Reverence for life, 10
Righteous gentiles, 55, 61
Righteousness, 39
  Moses and, 20–21
  Noah, 114
  non-Jews, 41, 55–58,
    131–132
  uniform standard, 53
Rivkah's, Rabbi Moshe, 213
Robbery, Seven Universal
    Laws of Noah, 169
Rogotchov, Rabbi Moshe
    (Rogotchover Gaon),
    213–214
Rosh Hashanah, 189, 190
  prayers for, 191–192
Royalty, non-Jewish, 38

Sabbath, 181
  prayer for, 196
Sacks, Rabbi Jonathan, 214
Salanter, Rabbi Yisrael, 214
Sanhedrin, 150

Schneerson, Rabbi Menachem
    Mendel, 214–215
Segregation, of Jews, 107
Segula, 138
Self-effacement, 147
Seven Universal Laws of Noah,
    165–167, 175
  basis for morality, 97
  blasphemy prohibited,
    167–168
  consuming live flesh pro-
    hibited, 170
  courts of justice established,
    167
  disseminating, 103–104
  history, 165–169
  idolatry prohibited, 168
  Jews as guarantors, 93,
    166–167
  kidnapping prohibited,
    168–169
  murder prohibited,
    168–169
  non-Jews, 45, 58, 61, 62,
    112
  robbery prohibited,
    168–169
  sexual immorality prohibited,
    168–169
  specified, 167–171
  taking a limb prohibited,
    169
Sexual immorality, Seven
    Universal Laws of Noah,
    169–170
Sforno, Rabbi Ovadyah, 215

Shavuos, 24, 101
Sins, forgiveness, 120
Sitna, 24
Slaughter, 170
Slavery, 22
Social activism, 20–21
Society, well-being of, 39–40
Solomon (King), 115–116
Soloveitchik, Rabbi Ahron,
    215
Speech, 94, 95
Stealing, 41–45, 48
    buying stolen goods, 44
    embezzlement, 44
    restitution, 41, 169
    Seven Universal Laws of
        Noah, 169
Sternhartz, Rabbi Nosson, 190,
    215–216
Stolen goods, buying, 44
Succos, 24, 78, 100, 101
Suffering, 15, 94, 122–123
Suicide, 169
Supernal Family, 27
Swords into ploughshares,
    159

Taharah, 177–178
Taking a limb, Seven Universal
    Laws of Noah, 170
Talmud, 216
Tax evasion, 38
Tefillin, 183–187
Ten Commandments, 115
Teshuvah, 101

Theft, 41–45, 48
    buying stolen goods, 44
    restitution, 41, 169
    Seven Universal Laws of
        Noah, 169
Three wells, 23–25
Tikkun, 113–116, 145
Tikkun olam, 93–97, 113
Torah d'Atika Stimah, 180
Torah, 175–181, 216
    crown of, 59–62
    dissemination of teachings,
        103–104, 107
    given in the dessert, 55
    in Messianic era, 180
    Messianic vision, 145–161
    protecting, 92
    purpose, 119, 175
    righteous converts, 65, 66
    study by non-Jews, 59–60,
        171
    tefillin, 183
    tzaddikim, hidden, 194–196
    universalism of, 107
    use of term adam, 131–136
    in written form, 95
Tosefos, 216
Tosefos Yom Tov (Rabbi Yom
    Tov Lipman Heller),
    216–217
Transgressions
    by non-Jews, preventing, 93
    Divine witness, 118
    of first ten generations, 113
    forgiveness, 120
    punishment for, 130

Travelers, 4, 16
Tribes, 141
Tzaddikim, hidden, 194–196
Tzedek, 20–21, 53

Ujheli, Rabbi Moshe Teitelbaum
  of, 217
Universal harmony, 109–110
Upper Unification, 185, 186

Vilna, Rabbi Pinchas Eliyahu,
  217
Vital, Rabbi Chaim, 217

War, 34
Wealth, Messianic era, 149
Wells, of Isaac, 23–25

Yaivi, Rav (Rabbi Yaakov Yosef
  of Ostrog), 218

Zebulun, 103
Zechariah, prophecy of, 110,
  155
Zohar, 185, 218
Zohar Chadash, 218

About the Author

David Sears is the author of *The Path of the Baal Shem Tov: Early Chasidic Teachings and Customs* (Jason Aronson Inc., 1997) and the author/illustrator of several Jewish children's books, the most recent of which is Rabbi Nachman's classic, *The Lost Princess* (Breslov Research 1996). Among his many interests is the preservation of traditional Jewish music. In 1991, he and Klezmer clarinetist/mandolinist Andy Statman founded Shoresh, an archive of traditional Jewish vocal and instrumental music. They have also coproduced several commercial recordings, including *Songs of the Breslever Chasidim: Today* (Aderet, 1993) and *Between Heaven and Earth: Music of the Jewish Mystics* (Shanachie, 1997). David and his wife, Shira, live in the Borough Park section of Brooklyn, NY.